Jerusalem the Golden

Jerusalem the Golden

Herman Douglas

Waymark Books

Copyright © 2022 by Waymark Books

This is an annotated edition of a public domain book.

CONTENTS

CHAPTER	vii
AUTHOR'S PREFIX	ix
MISS MANNING'S PREFIX	xi
INTRODUCTION	xxxiii

1 | A Sketch of the Holy Tabernacle and Its Vessels 1

2 | Proof from Scripture 40

3 | Progression of Glory 48

4 | Inexorable Division 59

5 | Symbolical Forms 84

6 | Symbolism of Sacred Vessels 113

7 | Jerusalem the Golden Foreshadowed by the Holy of Holies 149

THE MOST HOLY PLACE

AUTHOR'S PREFIX

The subject of the following pages formed the substance of two lectures which I delivered, in last March, at Reigate, in aid of the church which I have just completed for the benefit of "Londoners over the Border," among whom I have labored for nearly five years.

In publishing this volume, I yield more to the wishes of kind friends than to personal inclination; for, although the symbolism of the Tabernacle has long occupied me, I have neither leisure nor strength at present for careful writing.

The illustrations which accompany this book need as much indulgence as the text.

The designs for them were made by a much valued friend, from descriptions and rough sketches of mine, but were cut in wood before I had an opportunity of examining them.

If this volume should arrive at a second edition, the following corrections will have to be made:

1. The sketch of the general view of the Tabernacle will have to exhibit the tents of the Levites between the hangings of the Court and the Camp of Israel.

2. The Court of the Tabernacle would present a more correct view of the length of the Sanctuary; and the Cherubim which now

AUTHOR'S PREFIX

erroneously appear on the Vail of the Holy Place must be omitted, and replaced by foliage.

3. The dress of the High Priest, when in the Most Holy of the Tabernacle and Temple, must be white, and not consist as at present, of his *glorious robes*.

Yet notwithstanding these errors, I believe the illustrations will be useful, and I venture to send them forth in connection with the thoughts I have endeavored to express, *spe et oratione*.

H. Douglas
Custom-House Terrace
Victoria Docks, E.
Sept. 18, 1862

MISS MANNING'S PREFIX

It was early in the year that I was sitting, one fine afternoon, very happily engaged in collating *The Lady of La Garaye* with Cathenos' prose version of her story, when Mr. Douglas was announced. He had called about a fortnight before, to thank some of my Reigate friends, through me, for working for his poor people; and had then asked if he might call again.

I was very glad to see him, and said I had thought he must have returned to town.

"How could you think so," said he, "when I *said* I would come again?"

There was no answer for this; so I expressed a hope that he felt better for coming into the country.

He said, "Not at all."

I said, "Oh, but that is very ungrateful! You *ought* to feel better for coming into this pure, invigorating air!"

"I cannot get my poor people out of my head! I cannot sleep."

And then he asked me if he might talk to me about them; and when I said yes, he drew in his chair close to the fire, and sat looking into it while he told me of his poor people's sufferings and privations. There is relief, sometimes, in talking over what has much oppressed us, even if we do not know where to look for a remedy. I wrote down a good

MISS MANNING'S PREFIX

deal, afterwards, of what Mr. Douglas told me, because it touched me so much. He said:

> The Victoria Docks district is unlike any other about London. Almost all the people are poor, and the dock laborers are frequently out of work. When ships come up the river, many hands are wanted to unload them. Strength is the great desideratum; hence men who cannot get work elsewhere, flock to this market for their strength. A man comes to a little grating and calls out, 'A hundred hands (for example) are wanted.' The hundred hands are taken on; the rest are left to idle and starve. When the ships are unloaded, the extra hands are paid off. Thus, you see, it is almost like gambling—they never know when they shall have a job; they speculate on it, and become improvident.
>
> Then, again, we have many manufacturers, too offensive to be allowed in London—the vitriol works, the creosote works, the blood-manure manufacturer. The effluvium tells on our health, and has a very depressing influence. Awful casualties continually occur. I'll just give you an instance.
>
> A poor man went home one evening from the vitriol works, carrying all his earnings to his wife. As he was returning to his night-work, he was spoken to by some young men standing before a public house, who persuaded him to have some beer. He then went on to his work. He had to cross a plank, beneath which was a vat; he lost his balance, and fell in. By and by some workmen came, and began pouring vitriol into the vat. They found there was a man inside! He was taken out by shovelfuls!

The following was another of Mr. Douglas's instances:

> Philip, a dock laborer, fell ill, and I sent him to St. Thomas's Hospital. His family fared but badly during his seven weeks'

absence. At the end of that time he returned; and the very morning after he came back, he presented himself with hundreds of others at the dock gates. Being known there as a good laborer, he presently obtained a ticket through the lattice. The narrow gate which admits but one person at a time was thrown open by the dock policeman, and he marched off under his ganger to his task of unloading an East India ship freighted with rice. He thought himself a lucky fellow! Half-a-crown a day may seem but little to you, for a family to subsist upon, and not only to provide food, but clothing, shelter, and fire. Well, it's better than parochial relief, at any rate.

Ships are unloaded by means of heavy chains which are swung from hydraulic cranes at the height of more than forty feet; and the bags or chests engirdled by these chains are drawn up to the warehouse lofts. Philip was fastening the chain round the rice. Three bags were being drawn up together, when the hook at the top of the crane broke, as the rice swung midway between the ship and the loft—and the heavy chain, gathering momentum from the fall of the rice, struck him on the head and cleft that and his chest—*in twain*!

At four o'clock that afternoon, when the poor family expected Philip's return with his half-crown, they learnt that he was lying dead in one of the public-houses at the entrance of the docks. Was it not a mysterious providence that sent him to recover in hospital, and immediately on his return summoned him without a moment's warning into another world? Perhaps those seven weeks that were allotted him, of exemption from toil, and of the chaplain's ministrations, might have led him, poor fellow, to God.

Are you tired? Do I tire you? No? Thank you very much.

MISS MANNING'S PREFIX

I want to tell you about a poor man in the vitriol manufactory. He lived in a cottage adjoining the works. One Saturday afternoon, his wife woke him that he might go to his night-work. Instead of getting up, he put his arm round her neck, drew her head down to him, and, kissing her, said, 'I wish I had not to go to-night.' She laughed at him, and called him a lazy fellow: he laughed too, rose, kissed her again, kissed all the children, and saying some playful and kind words, left the house. Though he was always an affectionate fellow, yet somehow, this struck her—she was possessed with a strange and unaccountable sadness! On pretense of fetching water, she went out, hoping to see him in the yard. She could not do so, took her pail in, and again went into the yard, but again without success. Again she went in.

She had not been indoors ten minutes, when a lad rushed in—white! to tell her, almost inarticulately, that the fly-wheel had caught her husband, and whirling him round with tremendous velocity, had dashed him to pieces.

Had that poor creature had a *pre-sentiment*, think you? In a few days she wasted to a shadow. . . .

There was a man who was one of my most regular communicants. He and his family were very patterns of devout, industrious people. He had been manager of a railway belonging to an English company abroad. They all, especially his three daughters and two eldest boys, had learnt to speak French very well. I often had a pleasant little chat with them, and used to admire their fluency and correctness.

One Sunday night I observed them to be especially attentive. The chemist's only child had been buried during the week. I had baptized the child; and had afterwards looked on his sweet little face as he lay in his coffin. I had sympathized very much with the poor parents in their grief, and to comfort them had promised to preach a sermon for them.

My text was, 'I shall go to him; but he shall not return to me.' I felt much, and so did my congregation. T——'s family seemed particularly impressed. I had no idea, nor had they, that next Sunday *they* would be mourners.

The very next morning, while I was still in my dressing-room, a breathless messenger arrived to tell me that T—— had been drowned in the docks, and was then lying in the accident room. In a few minutes I was beside him. They had put him in a warm bath. The surgeon had opened a vein in his arm; but it would not bleed. I sent for my electric battery. We applied it in hopes of restoring animation; but in vain.

And then I had to break the news to the poor family. Oh, how *strong* the human heart must be that it can bear such shocks without breaking!

They had been one of the happiest, most united of families; and now their little household was broken up. T—— had earned good wages, and faithfully brought them home. His club gave the poor widow the means of burying him decently, and allowed her six shillings a week. Beyond that, she and her six children were suddenly penniless.

Stories such as these made me cease to wonder that Mr. Douglas "could not sleep at night for thinking of his poor people." There were sadder facts, relating to degradation and sin, that were greatly attributable to poverty, ignorance, and pernicious local influences.

An undrained marsh is Satan's seat. We read of an evil spirit roaming over dry places, seeking rest and finding none; that was no congenial soil for him! He had surer hope for work among poor wretches in unwholesome fenny districts.

From the continued breathing of a vitiated atmosphere inevitably arises either apathy or a craving for intoxicating drinks. To deliver the poor from these oppressive demons were a task worthy of the highest

MISS MANNING'S PREFIX

ambition. *(Cornhill Magazine, April, 1862. The surface of the marshes around the docks is imperfectly drained, and full of dykes and ponds, greener than grass. The area of houses in it is also drained now, but was not so when Mr. Douglas first came.)*

After a pause, I said, "I wish I could help you; but what can I do? I am not rich."

"I don't want your money—I want your pen."

"What can my pen do?"

"Write a story about my poor people."

"But the truth would be much more effective."

"Then write the truth. I can give you plenty of materials."

So this is why I am now writing.

I asked Mr. Douglas what was his most pressing object.

"To finish the church."

"How much is wanting?"

"Say, five hundred pounds. Another five hundred for the schools, a laundry for the ships' washing, a room for my wood-cutting boys."

"Stay—do not let us attempt too much. Let us try to do all we can to get the church open by Christmas."

And then we began to consider what we could do. Mr. Douglas said he had spent much money some years ago in having a beautiful model of the Tabernacle constructed, and that he should like to add to the funds for completing his church by lecturing on it. He had thought a great deal on the symbolic meaning of the Tabernacle, and had lectured on it already to his friends and his poor people. I undertook the arrangements for his lecturing in our beautiful new public hall, and wrote to many friends requesting their attendance.

In consequence of their kind response, the lecture was a brilliant success, and it led to arrangements being made that a second lecture should be given on the 21st of March.

The fall of snow on that day was the heaviest that had been known for years. The newspapers afterwards told us it lay so deep among the Mendip hills that roads were blocked up, and farmers prevented from going to market. Our hills were capped with white; and though St. Mark's bell rang for prayers, in the morning, nobody went but Mr. Douglas; so there was no service. It was very discouraging! But though the severity of the weather continued, there was an audience for the lecture.

There was not, indeed, a crowded hall. Some forty to fifty persons braved the inclemency of the night. I did not hear of any colds caught afterwards. For the sake of those who were not and could not be present, I am very glad that Mr. Douglas now publishes the lecture, which has, however, been recast; but, on comparing the short-hand notes with the lecture as it stands, I find nothing omitted that I could wish retained or added that does not make it better.

The time has' now come when the Lord's house—*this particular house*—should be built, that the church at the docks should be finished. Those generous persons who freely gave the money that has built two-thirds of it have a right to expect it. They have a right to expect that Mr. Douglas's voice should be heard in it, by the poor people for whom he has suffered so much, by next Christmas. *(Since writing the above, I have received the good news that there is every hope the church will be opened this August! A clergyman, full of strength and energy, has come forward*

MISS MANNING'S PREFIX

to take up and carry on Mr. Douglas' good works, and advance 600l. for the completion of the church. Another friend has promised an organ worth 400l. Thus, what represents 1000l is contributed by two persons; Mr. Douglas will have the rest he so much needs; his first wish is accomplished, and the chief want of remaining support of the industrial establishments for the profitable employment of women and boys, which is is hoped to obtain by a limited company.)

And here I would end this little preface did not Mr. Bentley, who has read it thus far, wish me to tell more about the poor people at the docks. That is easily done; though, to place them beside the beautiful Tabernacle, "with its bars, and its taches, and its rings," is very much like matching cloth of frieze with cloth of gold. It has seemed curious to me that so symbolical and spiritual a subject as the Tabernacle of Witness should have been thought out in such a locality as the Victoria Docks; and it reminded me of Ephraim Holding's reflections on seeing a delicate white bindweed trailing its blossoms beside a fetid, stagnant ditch.

First, for the locality.

"Few seem to know it," says Mr. Douglas, "if I may judge from the fact that a member of Parliament connected with the City asked last summer, whether we did not form part of the Isle of Dogs; which a leading periodical *answered in the affirmative*, though we are nearly as far east of the Isle of Dogs as that distinguished kennel is of Charing Cross. If you will kindly find Woolwich, in Kent, on your map, and look straight across the Thames, you will perceive, on the Essex or northern shore, a new settlement called North Woolwich, which forms the eastern boundary of my spiritual domain. From this point it stretches two miles west and about one mile north, right through the marshes."

The author of *Life Work* says:

I find it difficult to describe this district, it is *so dissimilar from every other*. . . . I can give no idea of the amount of its poverty and wretchedness; with *no house of relief except the cleryyman's*. None can walk through the unformed, muddy streets, without meeting many unfortunates of the lowest class—not hiding from day, but openly standing in groups on the path. The dwellings are like the people. I entered a house lately, and found a large hole in the flooring, with a board thrown carelessly across it, as the only preventive to five small children falling through to the basement. All their clothing consisted of thin, ragged, dirty frocks— poor half-starved, wretched little objects! and the look of hopeless ignorance, the filthy walls, the lack of furniture or comfort, told me that we had indeed reached the outcasts.

Mr. Douglas says:

In these depths I have been anxiously labouring for more than four years, assisted by a few devoted men and women—too few to do the difficult but glorious work effectually. The souls under my charge are about seven thousand, including, however, a *floating* population living on board ship in the Victoria Docks. I include these 'souls' on purpose, for I consider them as part and parcel of my care; and one of my Scripture readers visits every ship that is accessible to him, converses with the men who speak English, and distributes tracts and books, both in English and foreign languages.

Captains of our own and American trading vessels, their families, officers, and sailors, have attended the iron church, and return to us again on coming back to the Victoria Docks.*(Captains and the families, and crews, are informed that Divine Service is performed at the iron church close to the Tidal Basin Station every Sunday morning at 11 a.m., and every Sunday evening at half past 6 p.m., and that all sittings are free.— Circular)* One of these who seemed much impressed while here, wrote to me from various parts of the world. I last heard of him from the Brazils, and have since read his death in the papers.

Foreign sailors, too, who barely know English enough to follow our services, have occasionally attended; and I remember one poor fellow of very foreign aspect, who probably had not been in God's house for a long time, falling upon his knees and folding his hands in prayer, on entering one evening the porch of our little church.

It is grievous to see multitudes of foreign sailors walking about on Sunday as sheep without a shepherd. I wish we had a church for foreign sailors here, where service could be performed in Italian, Spanish, and German. Is not our country responsible to God for every soul that He, who orders the steps of all men, brings to our shores? Or are we content to send them back again to their distant homes without one effort to lead them to Christ? *(On one occasion, Mr. Douglas preached on the text, "There go the ships!")*

Our wants are pressing, and, in many cases, entirely exceptional; for, in the first place, the whole area now occupied by docks and dockyards, was, until recently, a marsh or swamp, kept from clean submersion by a close network of dykes and ditches, and the entire population, large as it is, seems to have sprung from the ground, like the fabled army of Aeacus. There was therefore no church to receive them, and no endowment. That both were imperatively required will not be called in question; and I thank God heartily that He has enabled me to commence and almost to complete a substantial church, and to secure a humble endowment.

In the next place, the great poverty of the population, dependent for subsistence on daily work, which often they cannot get for days and weeks together, rendered it equally imperative that means should be provided to prevent starvation in cases where the Poor-law is inoperative—as in the instance of able-bodied persons and their families; and in other cases, to augment the parochial allowance.

I will exemplify such cases presently.

But almost more than this, it was necessary to provide schooling for the children of both sexes; to give them a religious, secular, and industrial education, free of charge to the parents...

I have also felt it my duty to procure some work for the women, so as to enable them to earn a little when their husbands are entirely out of work, or unable to obtain sufficient work for maintenance.

I discourage the idea of women doing anything but household work, as it might lead worthless men to shirk work, and to live by the earnings of their wives, whom they are bound to support. In all these efforts I have been greatly encouraged by the excellent manager and superintendent of the docks, whose direct assistance and moral countenance are of the highest importance.

Besides all this, there are my regular services and my pastoral work; the latter, even with the help I have, is not inconsiderable. My work begins early in the morning, for my house is open to my poor—they often arrive before I have finished dressing. I see numbers of them daily, sometimes to give relief, or to procure work for them if possible, to supply them with hospital tickets, and to give them counsel; and I visit the sick and dying... This is no place for careless work! Our work must be done earnestly, and as if every man we speak to might not be seen again.

Here are one or two more cases he added:

I have visited a mother and son, both dying of consumption. In the boy it was probably hereditary; but it was brought on in a very melancholy way. He was employed in the ship-building yard as a riveter. One day, after some hours' hard work, with fiery rivets, he sat down, still streaming with perspiration, under a doorway. The 10 ft above was constructed of planks laid side by side to form a gangway. In that loft some of his older companions were sitting, eating their cold meat and bread, which they cut with their pocket-knives.

One of them, observing the boy below, emptied a can of cold water upon him. It gave him a chill which, in a few months, led to his death. I often sat beside him and his mother, who lay in one bed, and died in it.

Another lad, who was brutally kicked by an older mate, was laid up, in consequence, with a tumor, of which he languished in his father's house nearly two years. This cruel act led to a prosecution, and the offender had to pay ten pounds damages. The boy died last autumn, after great and prolonged sufferings.

'I fully, freely forgive the man who hurt me,' he said. 'I was a wicked lad, and used to swear and do many wrong things. God has led me to repentance, and I humbly hope I am forgiven through Jesus Christ.'

A poor fellow lodges close to us who has been in the Consumption Hospital, and returned better, but has since lost ground again, though he continues to work for himself and family. He has a wife and child to support, but it is not much that he can bring them, for his energetic mind is coupled with a sadly enfeebled body. Port wine and cod-liver oil are almost necessary to his existence. Could he get a lighter employment, he would suffer less.

He was one of the soldiers sent by the East India Company to hunt after Nana Sahib. At Cawnpore he was wounded in both arms, and had no other drink than water mingled with blood. In Delhi he was on garrison duty, where he fell ill of fever produced by the stench of putrefying bodies; and was sent on sick leave to the mountains, where he recovered. Of the 360 men who had gone out to India with him, only nine lived to return. Numbers died on the homeward voyage; he returned to his mother, and spent all his savings before he was strong enough to work. 'I was reduced to that state,' he said, 'that when I got money to buy a piece of meat, my taste for it was gone; it might as well have been a piece of wood.'

Let us hear the voices of some of these poor people themselves. Their stories are very touching. Last year, a statement appeared in the *Times* that the poor of Victoria Docks district were in such urgent want, that several women near their confinement were in literal want of food. On this, a correspondent inquired what the Poor-law authorities were about, if such things were true. This drew the attention of the Select Committee of the House of Commons; and its Chairman, the Right Hon. Charles Pelham Villiers, who was also President of the Poor-law Board, desired that an inspector should be present at the next meeting of the Board of Guardians of the West Ham Union. In consequence of this inspector's report, Mr. Douglas desired to appear before the Select Committee, and produce a statement on his own part; which he did on the 4th of June.

On this occasion, he cited twenty-eight cases, corroborating the original statement in the *Times*.

This led to an inquiry before Sir John Walsham, by whom the cases were examined. All I have to give is the picture of these poor people's privations, and their preference of almost any hardship to going into "the house," relieved here and there by sweet touches of family love.

MISS MANNING'S PREFIX

First, a seafaring man is examined.

"You are of the Victoria Docks district?"

"Yes."

"What are you by business?"

"I'm in the sailoring line, and work at rigging-work, or anything in the docks."

"Are you married?"

"Yes."

"Is your wife alive?"

"She was, when I left home this morning."

"How many children have you?"

"Seven."

"How are you off, as to employment?"

"I have no constant employment; only casual jobs. All this year since Christmas I have been very slack indeed."

"Can you give me any idea of your average wages since Christmas?"

"I would not venture to say that I have earned more than nine shillings a week."

"Have you been any weeks without anything to do at all?"

"Several weeks since Christmas."

"About the time your wife was confined, was work very slack?"

"I had scarcely anything to do for a fortnight."

"Did you make any application to the relieving officer?"

"Yes."

"What passed between you?"

"I asked him for relief. I told him my children were at the present time wanting bread. He said he could not help it: he had orders from the gentlemen not to relieve any able-bodied persons; but, if in a starving state, to send them to Mr. Douglas."

"Did he not let you know you might have an order for the house?"

"He said something about that, but I did not much regard it; because that was cold relief for hungry, starving children."

"But your children would have been well fed and clothed, if they had come into the house."

"On a dark and cold night, with snow on the ground, I believe, what could I have done with six starving children? I would sooner have gone round the neighborhood."

"Did you tell Mr. —— that your wife was about to be confined?"

"I can't exactly tell the words I said to him."

"When he knew it, did he make any observation?"

"No."

"Then, you had no relief when your wife was confined?"

"Yes, I had!—God sent me a friend—the Rev. Mr. Douglas."

A poor woman is examined; the wife of a dock laborer. She has four children, from six years to four months old. She applied for relief in that severe January, just before her confinement, when her husband had smashed his toe. It was a very bad day; her shoes were worn out, but she had no one to go for her, and she was almost starving. She sat down, very ill, on a doorstep. Neither she nor her children had tasted food that day. She got an order for eighteen-pennyworth of grocery, the same amount in meat, and three loaves, which was to be continued four weeks.

It was very wet and very muddy: she had to sit down on the stairs when she returned, or she would have fallen; it was some time before she could get up.

"How long did the relief last? About four weeks?"

"Yes, but my husband asked for more the second week of my confinement."

"Was he laid off work all the time?"

"Yes, all the time."

"Had he no club?"

"No club whatsoever."

"Then, what you had to live on was what you had from the parish?"

"And what I had from Mr. Douglas."

She had not been confined, however, in Mr. Douglas's district, but had been moved into it on the ninth day, because the house over her head had been sold."

"All the neighbors left—the street was completely empty at once."

At the three weeks' end she had to leave her baby and go for relief herself.

"There was nobody we could ask to go but my landlady, and she had five children. My husband had to go once for it. He had to take a stick with him and go along the best way he could, by the palings. The doctor ordered me a nurse, but I was not allowed one. If it had not been for Mrs. Douglas's nurse, baby and me must have been lost."

"Was any reason given why a nurse was not allowed?"

"No; only that my husband was at home, and he might manage for me."

"It seems that the 22nd of February was on a Friday. That was the last week your husband received relief. Did he go to work —or try to go to work—three or four days before that?"

"On the Monday he tried to go to work in the docks; but he could not work. He had to come home and take off his stocking, and the nail came off his toe." ("Surely these are poor." Jer. 5:4)

Mr. Douglas here said:

> I think the question seems to proceed on the supposition that some charge has been made, either against the Board or against the medical officer. Now, I emphatically deny that any such charge has been made; and I beg to say, once and for all, that I have made no such charge and intended none. I merely said that there was relief necessary besides what was given.
>
> And I think we may say the same. A poor woman next comes up whose husband worked "off and on" at the docks, but was very frequently "off." He had been very unfortunate of late. Their

little girl had been "very bad with abscess in the throat." She applied for relief, and got a shilling's worth of meat.

A lady came in at the time baby was lying ill in my arms. She said, "What is the matter with your baby?' I said, "She is very bad." She said, "Mr. Douglas has a nurse; I will send her down."

She went back to Mr. Douglas. Mr. Douglas sent a bottle of port wine and some beef-tea; so I continued on till the baby got well with the port wine and the beef-tea.

"The port wine and the beef-tea that you got from Mr. Douglas?"

"From Mr. Douglas; and also he kept me in bread and things till the child got well; or else she would have been in her grave now, I do believe."

Another poor woman comes up, a native of Manchester, her clothing of the poorest.

"You appear to have been in a great deal of distress?"

"We have been, indeed."

"Are you at all better off now?"

"A little better; my husband is doing a little more."

"You have rather a heavy family still?"

"Four."

"You have lost a good many?"

"Yes."

"It appears, however, that though you were in such serious distress you did not make any application to the parish?"

"No; I made none at all, because I thought it was only for the sick."

"Do you not know that every person that is destitute may have relief of some kind or other?"

"No; I have never had any relief at all, except from Mr. Douglas . . . We did not wish to come into the house; my husband was in his health and strength, and did not wish to come."

Surely the repugnance did credit to our national character. And yet every means is taken to break it down: to put those who would get work but cannot on the same level as those who could get work but will not.

Another:

"What is your husband?"

"A fitter and millwright."

"You have a large family?"

"We have."

"You seem to have been, when your last child was born, in rather a sad condition?"

"I was indeed."

"And you had assistance from Mr. Douglas?"

"I had."

"You pawned a good many things?"

"I pawned everything, I may say."

"Your husband is a little better off now—in work?"

"Yes; he has got into the police in the docks. That is through Mrs. Douglas getting him on there; he went three days after my confinement."

She is asked if she had any particular reason for not applying to the parish. Yes; she knew the only remedy offered would be to go into the house.

She knew she should be separated there from her husband and children. She thought she would rather do almost anything than be parted from them.

"Don't you think you would be quite as independent receiving relief in this house as receiving it of Mr. Douglas?"

"No, I do not; because my husband has been at liberty to seek for work."

Another witness, a poor man, bursts out with: "I love my wife and children! and therefore, as I told Mr.—— , in my own house, before I would be parted from my children and from my wife, I would put an end to all our existence at once."

Sir John calmed him down by telling him that this expression was really very improper and wrong, continuing:

> For after all being said and done, although it is not a desirable thing for any person to come into the workhouse, you should really consider what the workhouse is—a good house, good clothing, and education for your children, and you can walk out of it the very moment you feel disposed.
>
> And as to separation, begging your pardon, it is all humbug, because we are all separated from our children in every grade in life: they are obliged to be knocked about and separated from us. They go to school and to every part of the world; and that braggadocio way of talking about putting an end to your children's

lives, rather than they should be clothed and fed and educated, when you are distressed yourself, and cannot maintain them, as you are bound to do if you can, on account of your being unfortunate enough not to get work, is exceedingly wrong—very foolish talking indeed; very wrong talking.

And Mr. Douglas says so too; and we feel the poor man was wrong, and he feels it himself, and says he only said that, on the impulse of the moment, because he was overcome by his feelings.

Well, we take pains, on principle, in the first instance, to make the unions so arid, so untempting, that even vagrants will only resort to them on necessity; and then we take all this trouble to coax, to compel, to force into them our respectable, domestic, unfortunate poor, who naturally "recoil from swelling the list of the *seven hundred thousand* who are put aside in them as in a living grave, as respects all the sweet humanities and charities of life, the sympathy of kindly looks and words.*(Mrs. G. W. Sheppard's Sunshine in the Workhouse." After visiting in our own workhouse ever since 1850, I feel that I can do no less than state my corroborating experience of the fact, that while the English workhouses are fitting abodes for those who can work and will not, yet as asylums for the aged, the infirm, the crippled, and the incapable poor, whether old or young, they are sadly deficient in the loving charity which should make the pauper's last earthly home a quiet, happy, cheerful one."—Ibid. "Let it be a home, not a prison, for those who have committed no offense against society, and who have perhaps spent their best years in laboring for its wants." —Mr. Pownall's pamphlet on the Maintenance of the Aged and the Necessitous Poor.)* That is one great evil. Another is, that, conscious we have 'stripped these refuges of every attraction till:

> One by one
> The sweetnesses of life are gone.

MISS MANNING'S PREFIX

We are ashamed to let people see what they really are, and jealously exclude gentle and simple, till they have the same vague dread of the interior as of the inside of Bedlam. This at least might be remedied. Every one who has read the plague-scenes in *I Promessi Sposi* can remember the creeping chill with which they approached the fated hospital, within whose walls were passing unimaginable horrors.

When we got within them, what did we find? Death, indeed, and agony, exhaustion, and pain, but sweet alleviations of tenderness, sisters of mercy assuaging suffering, young girls ministering to the aged and helpless, goats suckling many an innocent little Romulus and Remus whom the fell pestilence had orphaned. Were the poor freely shown such ministrants inside our unions, and were those whom God has joined and set in families not sundered, would they shrink from them in such dismay?

A. M.

P.S. The church is now consecrated, but the completion cost more than was anticipated, and 500i. are still wanted to clear it of debt.

INTRODUCTION

Alone with God on Mount Sinai, and in such absorbing communion with Him, that for the space of forty days and forty nights, during which that communion lasted, he neither ate bread nor drank water, Moses saw in visions, which may possibly have been protracted through the entire period, that temple which is known to us as the prototype of the Holy Tabernacle.

And while that divine temple stood revealed before he received a most minute explanatory description of its details, and the command to erect its material copy among his people.

Whether a revelation so wonderful and impressive required a further miraculous supervision when Moses recorded it, may be left to conjecture; but it is absolutely certain that on his descent from the mountain, he communicated the divine plan to his artificers, word for word.

And God's agency connected with the origin of the Tabernacle ended not with the mere revelation of its plan. So lofty a conception demanded inspired men for its embodiment, and these the Lord provided.

He said to Moses:

> "See, I have called by name
> Bezaleel the son of Uri, the son of Hur, of the tribe of Judah:
> And I have filled him with the spirit of God,
> In wisdom, and in understanding, and in knowledge,

INTRODUCTION

> And in all manner of workmanship,
> To devise cunning works,
> To work in gold, and in silver, and in brass,
> And in cutting of stones, to set them,
> And in carving of timber,
> To work in all manner of workmanship.
> And I, behold, I have given with him
> Aholiab of the tribe of Dan:
> And in the hearts of all that are wise-hearted
> I have put wisdom,
> That they may make all that I have commanded thee;
> The Tabernacle of the Congregation,
> And the Ark of the Testimony. (Exodus 31:1-11)

The names of these two men, given probably in allusion to their moral character, seem suggestive; for Bezaleel signifies "under the shadow of the Mighty," as if to indicate that the artificer had habitually lived in God's presence, as it is written:

"He that dwelleth in the secret place of the Most High, Shall abide under the shadow of the Almighty," (Psalm 41:1) and Aholiab denotes "The Father is my tent" as if to declare that he also had lived in this high communion.

To these two men the fulness of God's Spirit was vouchsafed for the execution of their task, and a supernatural emulation to aid them spread rapidly through the entire people:

> "And they came, both men and women,
> As many as were willing-hearted,
> And brought bracelets, and earrings, and rings, and tablets,
> All jewels of gold...
> And every man, with whom was found blue,

> And purple, and scarlet,
> And fine linen, and goats' hair brought them.
> And all the women that were wisehearted
> Did spin with their hands,
> And brought that which they had spun,
> Both of blue, and of purple, and of scarlet, And of fine linen...
> And the rulers brought onyx stones,
> And stones to be set,
> For the ephod, and for the breast-plate;
> And spice and oil..." (Exodus 35:22-28)

So freely and cheerfully gave they their treasures and their labor, that Moses was compelled to restrain them.

> "And he gave commandment,
> And they caused it to be proclaimed
> Throughout the camp, saying,
> Let neither man nor woman make any more work
> For the offering of the sanctuary.
> So the people were restrained from bringing.
> For the stuff they had was sufficient for all the work to make it,
> And too much." (Exodus 36:5-7)

And when at last the structure and its vessels were completed and brought for inspection and approval to the prophet who had seen their prototype in holy vision, it is said:

> "And Moses did look upon all the work,
> And, behold, they had done it as the Lord had commanded,
> Even so had they done it:
> And Moses blessed them." (Exodus 39:3)

Such, then, was the origin of the Mosaic Tabernacle.

INTRODUCTION

In the unspeakable sublimity of a purely divine conception, wrought out in faultless forms by inspired hands, it towered in immeasurable significance above all mere human temples; and its faithful description is doubtless preserved to us to challenge devout inquiry into its meaning.

It may be very difficult to determine whether the prototype of the Tabernacle which Moses saw on that high mountain be identical with the Tabernacle of Witness which, many centuries after, the great Prophet of the New Testament beheld.

But it is certain that the Most Holy Place of the Mosaic Tabernacle bore a remarkable resemblance to what John saw in vision when the angel carried him away in the spirit to a great and high mountain, and showed him that great city—the New Jerusalem descending out of heaven from God. (Revelation 15:5, 21:10)

This I hope to show in the sequel, and also that the other portions of the Holy Tabernacle and their sacred vessels foreshadowed the way in which we must strive to attain to the Golden City. I now proceed to describe the Mosaic structure and its vessels.

1

A Sketch of the Holy Tabernacle and Its Vessels

The Tabernacle stood due east and west. Its entrance was from the east; so also, the entrance of the Holy Temple at Jerusalem. It formed a rectangle, or right-angled parallelogram, and consisted of three divisions: The Court, the Holy Place, and the Most Holy.

The Court

The Court (*See Note A*) was one hundred cubits long, fifty broad, and five cubits high. The ancient Hebrew cubit is said to have been twenty-one inches and a half.

But as Herodotus made a distinction between the vulgar and the royal ell (*measurement*), saying that the latter exceeded the former by three fingers' breadth, so the Rabbins distinguish between a common and sacred cubit; and R. Simeon Ben Jochai mentions that the sacred cubit contained six palms, and, if the palm, as is usually believed, was twelve inches, the cubit measured six feet.

It is also said that the common shekel was only one half of the shekel of the Sanctuary; and if the cubit of the Sanctuary differed from the other in the same manner, it would. at least have been twice twenty-one inches and a half.

But as this is uncertain, I am content to assume that the Mosaic cubit was in round numbers equal to two feet of our measurement, and that the Court was therefore two hundred feet long, one hundred broad, and ten feet high.

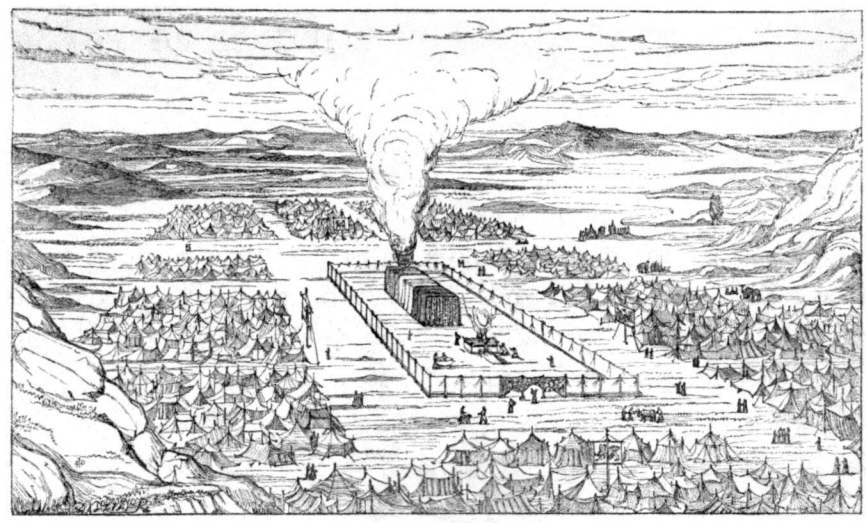

GENERAL VIEW OF THE TABERNACLE AND ITS SURROUNDING ENCAMPMENT

It was formed by means of sixty pillars—twenty of which stood north, twenty south, ten east, and ten west. A space of five cubits, or ten feet, was left between pillar and pillar, and they were made of shittim, or, as the Septuagint has translated it, of imperishable wood. (*Josephus called these pillars "brazen," but there is no ground for it in Holy Scripture—as little as for his other assertion, that the four pillars of the gate were of silver. Shittim may have been the Acacia Arabica, which as late as S. Jerome abounded in the Desert of Sinai (Hieron. in Micha, 6:5). He says also, it was exceedingly strong, light, and imperishable—of incredible lightness and beauty (in Isaiah 41:19; Joel 3:18). Herodotus speaks, it seems to me, of the same wood as used by the Egyptians in shipbuilding (2:95); and*

JERUSALEM THE GOLDEN

Pliny (Hist. Nat. 13:9) says of the Acacia, that it was celebrated for being imperishable. Dr. Livingstone found a similar tree in Africa—Acacia Giraffe. He says: "It is probable that this is the tree of which the Ark of the Covenant and the Tabernacle were constructed, as it is reported to be found where the Israelites were at the time these were made. It is an imperishable wood." Durandus says: "Its leaves are like the whitethorn, and to be injured neither by fire nor decay." His authority I do not know. Our poplar also is said not to be easily ignited).

Each pillar was five cubits in height, stood in a socket of brass which was embedded in the soil, and was crested with silver. Underneath each silver crest was a hook of silver, from which curtains of fine white byssus (*silk or linen*) were suspended, which enclosed the Court. These hangings, Josephus says, gave the exterior of the Court the appearance of a wall; and this resplendent wall with its gleaming silver crests reminds one involuntarily of the jasper, or, as modern critics have it, the diamond wall which surrounds the heavenly city in the Apocalypse.

The Court-Gate

At the eastern extremity of the Court hung a white Vail (*See Note B*) twenty cubits broad and five long, embroidered with crimson, purple, and blue. It was suspended on four pillars and formed the entrance from the camp. The pattern of the embroidery in the Vail is not named in Holy Scripture, but is believed to have consisted of foliage and flowers. And it is curious that, in describing the embroidery of the Tabernacle and of the vestments of its ministers, the Scriptures make use of two different words: the one, according to the Talmud, denoting that the pattern was seen on one side only; the other, that the pattern appeared on both sides: and the first term is used with remarkable precision when describing the Vail of the Court, of the Holy Place, and the girdle of the common priest; the second when speaking of the richer and more beautiful workmanship of the Vail of the Most Holy, the lowermost curtain which formed the roof of the Tabernacle, and the girdle and ephod of the high priest.

The Court had no roof, but was overshadowed by day by a miraculous cloud, which mitigated the heat and glare of the sun; and changing into a pillar of fire as night came on, illumined the Court and camp when the outlying desert was wrapped in darkness.

And this cloud it was which guided the Israelites through their wanderings for forty years.

> "And when the cloud was taken up from over the tabernacle,
> The children of Israel went onward in all their journeys:
> But if the cloud were not taken up, then they journeyed not till
> The day that it was taken up.
> For the Cloud of the Lord was upon the tabernacle by day,
> And fire was on it by night,
> In the sight of all the house of Israel,
> Throughout all their journeys." (Exodus 40:36-38)

The Tabernacle Proper

Towards the middle of the Court rose the Tabernacle proper (*See Note C*), which was divided into the Holy Place and the Most Holy. It was constructed of forty-eight square pillars of imperishable wood, each pillar being ten cubits high, one and a half broad, and probably one cubit deep. They had each two tenons or hooks, which were set into pairs of morticed sockets or bases of pure silver, each single base weighing one talent, or one hundred and fourteen pounds. The pillars stood close to each other—twenty north, twenty south, and eight in the west. They were covered over with fine gold, had three rows of rings (*some have depicted the Tabernacle with five rows of bars, but they have mistaken the fact that the upper and lower rows were—for symbolic reasons probably—cut in two, for a command to make five bars*) externally, into which strong bars of wood covered with gold were thrust on the three sides, so as to keep them true to each other.

Its Curtains

The entire length of the two divisions, measuring internally thirty cubits by ten in breadth and ten in height, was roofed in by four overhanging curtains. The dimensions of these curtains, the materials of which they were composed, the manner in which they were joined together, and the order in which they lay one above the other, formed matter of special and minute revelation. But as it is only my intention to notice broad results in my attempt to explain the symbolical meaning of this structure, I am content with sketching its general outlines. I shall not pause, therefore, to describe the mystic dimensions, nor the mystic unions effected in these curtains; but deem it sufficient to say that the lowest of the four overhanging curtains (*See Note D*) was made of fine white linen, embroidered with red, purple, blue, and with Cherubim, in the rich and costly manner of the third Vail and the ephod of the high priest, and that it formed the ceiling of the Holy and Most Holy places, and covered the golden walls of both divisions.

Some writers, and not without show of reason, have maintained that this beautiful curtain hung outside the golden walls. This is possible, though in this case the Cherubim would not have been seen on the interior walls of the Holy and Most Holy places, being concealed between the three remaining curtains and the gold-covered pillars.

But the point, whether the curtain formed the drapery of the Sanctuaries, or hung between the exterior of the walls and the overlying curtains, affects not the great symbolical lesson which the curtain was intended to convey.

Over this embroidered curtain lay another of finest white goats' hair, combed from the fleece of kids. It was soft, like silk, and shone like polished silver. Above this lay a third, of rams' skins dyed red or crimson, and over it a fourth made of tachash—or, as we have translated it, of badgers' skins, but which others have rendered the skins of dolphins—dolphins abounding in the Red Sea. (*This notion was probably current in Herod's time; for on the base of the candlestick which was sculptured on the Arch of Titus, and is supposed to be a likeness of the candlestick he took from the Temple, dolphins are represented*).

But the tachash seems to have been the name of some skin which was either peculiarly adapted for blue dye, or which was always dyed blue.

The *Septuagint* translates the word simply hyacinthine. St. Jerome, in Ezekiel 16:10, renders it sky-blue; and Josephus supports this rendering when he speaks of blue-dyed skins being used in the construction of the Tabernacle.

He says:

> "The Israelites rejoiced, . . . and were not wanting in diligence according to their ability; for they brought silver, and gold, and brass, and of the best sorts of wood, such as would not at all decay; camels' hair also, and sheep skins, some of them dyed of a blue color, and some of a scarlet . . . for of these materials did Moses build the tabernacle." *(Ant. b. iii. c. 6, § 1)*

Seen from the camp or the distant desert, the Tabernacle appeared of dazzling white, the emblem of purity, and bright Cerulean blue, the emblem of heaven, and it was overshadowed by the symbol of the Divine presence and goodness.

The Vail of the Most Holy Place

The entrance from the Court to the Holy Place was formed by a Vail (*See Note E*) ten cubits square, but precisely similar in texture, color, and embroidery to the Vail of the Court.

It hung on five pillars of shittim-wood cased in fine gold, but resting, like the pillars of the Court, in sockets of brass. The Holy Place was twenty cubits long, ten broad, and ten high; and at its western extremity stood four pillars sheathed in fine gold, and set in sockets of pure silver. On these pillars hung the beautiful Vail (*See Note F*) which separated the Holy from the Most Holy.

The Most Holy Place

The shape of the latter was a cube—ten cubits high, ten broad, and ten deep.

Such are the brief outlines of the three divisions of the Holy Tabernacle.

I now proceed to sketch as rapidly the sacred vessels.

In describing the vessels which God commanded to be placed in the Tabernacle, I shall reverently invert the order in which they are mentioned in Holy Scripture, and begin with those of the Court, instead of the Ark of the Covenant, with which the Scriptures commence the enumeration.

The Laver

First in the Court, and nearest the entrance from the camp, stood the Laver (*See Note G*). This must not be confounded with the Molten Sea, which was of much later origin, and stood in the Court of Solomon's Temple.

Many persons place the Laver second, not first, in the Court; and I feel therefore bound to state my grounds for the deviation. They are as follows:

1st. The priests were solemnly forbidden to approach the Altar, or to enter the Holy Place on pain of death, unless they had first washed in the Laver (*See Preceding Note*). It is therefore most reasonable to assume that the Laver, the very object of which was to prepare them to approach the "Most Holy Altar," should have met them at their very entrance into the Court.

2ndly. We may safely assume that the Altar of Burnt-offering in the Tabernacle, and the Altar of Burnt-offering in the Temple, stood in the same relative position to the Holy Place and the Laver.

The Altar

Now in reference to this Altar in the Temple, it is certain that nothing stood between it and the entrance into the Holy Place. Thus, Ezekiel says:

> "He brought me
> Into the inner court of the Lord's House,
> And, behold, *at the door of the Temple of the Lord,*
> *Between the Porch and the Altar,*
> Were about five-and-twenty men,
> With their backs towards the Temple of the Lord,
> And their faces towards the east;
> And they worshipped the sun toward the east." (Ezekiel 8:16)

Clearly nothing intervened here between the door of the Temple or the porch, and the Altar, save the five-and-twenty men of whom the prophet speaks. Had the Laver stood between the Altar and the Temple, the five-and-twenty men must have been seen between the Temple door and the Laver, and not, as they were, between the Temple door and the Altar.

Similar to this are the expressions in Joel:

> "Let the priests, the ministers of the Lord,
> Weep between the porch and the altar." (Joel 2:17)

And in Matthew and Luke, where our Lord says:

> "Wherefore, behold, I send unto you Prophets,
> And wise men and Scribes;
> And some of them ye shall kill and crucify;
> That upon you may come all the righteous blood
> Shed upon the earth,
> From the blood of righteous Abel
> Unto the blood of Zacharias, son of Barachias,
> Whom ye *slew between the Temple and the Altar.*"
> (Matthew 23:35; Luke 11:51; comp. with 2 Chronicles 24:21)

The obvious inference from these passages is that the space between the Temple door and the Altar was free, and that the Laver stood not between. It may, however, have stood sideways, and the testimony of Jewish writers says so expressly, stating at the same time that it was placed nearer the entrance of the Court than the Altar, and was therefore the first object which met the priest as he entered for the performance of his functions.

Thus Jarchi, who quotes the *Talmud Sebachim*, in his support, and Aben-Ezra, 1n Exodus 30:13, 19. They place it at the south side of the Court.

But, 3rdly, it should never have been overlooked, that in the repeated enumerations of the sacred vessels found in Exodus, from the twenty-fifth to the fortieth chapter, the Scriptures invariably begin with the Ark of the Covenant and end with the Laver; and in four instances out of the five in which this is done, the enumeration commences with the Ark, proceeds to the Holy Table, the Golden Candlestick, the Altar of Incense, the Altar of Burnt-Offering, and closes with the Laver. The following is one instance out of the four in the language of the Scriptures:

> "And they brought the tabernacle unto Moses,
> The tent, and all his furniture . . .
> The ark of the testimony, and the staves thereof,
> And the mercy seat,
> The table, and all the vessels thereof . . .
> The pure candlestick, with the lamp thereof . . .
> And the golden altar,
> And the anointing oil,
> And the sweet incense,
> And the hanging for the tabernacle door,
> The brazen altar, and his grate of brass, . . .
> The laver and his foot." (Exodus 39:33-39)
> *(See also Exodus 30:7-9, 37, 38, 40:21-30)*

I conclude, therefore, that the Laver stood farthest from the Ark of all the sacred vessels, and that as the Ark of the Covenant stood in the last and highest place in the Mystical Temple, so the Laver occupied the first and lowest; and as the Ark was seen only at the end and termination, so the Laver stood at its very entrance.

What has misled writers on this subject, apart perhaps from a certain doctrinal bias, is the expression—"He set the Laver between the Tent of the Congregation and the Altar" (Exodus 40:30), and they take for granted that the Tent of the Congregation signifies the Tabernacle proper. It certainly does mean it sometimes, nay frequently, but not always, and often denotes the Court. (*"And when they shall blow with them [the trumpets], All the assembly shall assemble themselves to thee at the door of the Tabernacle [Ohel=Tent] of the congregation."* Numbers 10:3).

It is scarcely necessary to remind the attentive reader that 600,000 men could not have stood within the Court, the free space of which measured little over 110 feet in length, and 100 in breadth; that therefore the door here spoken of must have been that of the gate of the Court, not of the Holy Place.

So also, in the following passages:

> "And they took every man his censer,
> And put fire in them,
> And laid incense thereon,
> And stood in the door of the
> Tabernacle [Ohel=Tent] of the congregation . . .

At best, then, the term is doubtful, sometimes denoting the Court, at other times the Sanctuary; and when the considerations which I have pointed out are fairly weighed, I doubt not but the balance will be felt to incline towards the place which I have ventured to assign to the Laver.

Its size and shape are not given in the Scriptures, but the latter is supposed to have been hemispherical, as it were a hollow ball cut in two, and its convex base was placed upon a pedestal or column.

The Rabbins imagining that to wash in it must have defiled the water it contained, alleged that some contrivance was added which caused the water to flow over the hands and feet of the persons who performed their preparatory ablutions. But this is a later idea, the result of their views of Tumah, or ceremonial impurity.

The Mosaic records say nothing of the kind; but they tell us expressly that the material of which the Laver was constructed was derived from:

> "The looking-glasses of the women which assembled at the door of the Tent of the Congregation." (Exodus 38:8)

That we have to think here of metal mirrors is plain; for glasses were not invented for more than two thousand years after, and the Laver is distinctly said to have been made of brass, or lit. of copper.

Metal mirrors only were anciently known, and were used in Egyptian worship. (*It is said that Genesis 44:5, contains an allusion to the use of concave mirrors by the Egyptian sorcerers*).

The metal thus employed was capable of being highly polished, and the Laver might serve as a solemn memento to the entering priests, to warn them of their need of inward purity.

Mirrors seem to have been used for this purpose also in later heathen temples. A traveler in Japan relates:

> "In the Centre of their temples are found frequently huge mirrors of cast and polished metal, whose object it is to remind all who enter, that, as the mirrors reflect faithfully all defects of the body, so all secret faults and evil dispositions of the mind are naked and open to the eyes of the all-seeing and immortal gods."— *Thunbuery,* quoted by Bahr, *Symb. d. m. Cult.* i. 497.

> *"And Korah gathered all the congregation against them unto the door of the Tabernacle [Ohel=Tent] of the congregation." (Numbers 16:19)*

> *"And behold, one of the children of Israel came*

In the sight of all the congregation of the children of Israel,
Who were weeping
Before the door of the Tabernacle [Ohel=Tent] of the congregation."
(Numbers 25:6)

"And they stood before Moses,
And before Eleazar, the priest,
And before the princes
And all the congregation,
By the door of the Tabernacle
[Ohel=Tent] of the congregation." (Numbers 27:2)

"Then a cloud covered
The Tent [Ohel] of the congregation,
And the glory of the Lord Filled the Tabernacle
[Mishcan—literally, the Sanctuary]." (Exodus 40:34)'

Here, then, a distinction is made between the Tent of the Congregation, and the Tabernacle proper, and the Sanctuary; and Tent obviously means the Court. And this distinction is repeated, when it is said again:

"And Moses was not able to enter
Into the Tent [Ohel] of the congregation,
Because the cloud abode thereon,
And the glory of the Lord filled the Tabernacle [Mishcan]."
(Exodus 40:35)

But the mystic cloud retired to the roof of the Mishcan, or Sanctuary:

"And when the cloud was taken up from over the Mishcan [Tabernacle],
The children of Israel went onward in their journeys:
For the cloud of the Lord
Was upon the Tabernacle [Mishcan] by day. . . " (Exodus 40:36, 38)

> "When they went into The Tent [Ohel] of the congregation,
> And when they came near unto the altar,
> They washed..." (Exodus 40:32)

This distinction between Court under the appellation of Ohel, or Tent of the congregation, extends into a much later period—e.g.:

> "And that they who keep the charge
> Of the Tabernacle [Ohel] of the congregation,
> And the charge of the Holy Place." (1 Chronicles 23:32)

These are some of the instances in which the phrase "Tent of the congregation" clearly and distinctly denotes the Court.

The Brazen Altar

(*See Note H*).

Between the Laver and the entrance into the Holy Place, probably before the Vail of the Holy Place, stood the Brazen Altar, or the Altar of Burnt-offering. This Altar in the Court of the Tabernacle was five cubits in length and breadth, and three in height; but the Altar in Solomon's Temple was twenty cubits in length and breadth, and ten cubits in height. Both altars were too high for the performance of service upon them without an ascent. In the Tabernacle a ledge or "settle" on the Altar served this purpose. The Altar of the Temple was approached by an inclined plane on the south side. Three fires are said to have burnt continually on the Altar in the Temple (*Ioma, iv.5; R. Juda Leon. lib.ii. De Temple, c. xiii. § 76, seq.*), but only one on the Altar in the Tabernacle. The fire of both these altars had fallen from Heaven, and was never quenched, and probably unquenchable by rain. (Leviticus 9:23, 24; 2 Chronicles 7:1)

The Altar in the Tabernacle was made of shittim-wood carefully encased in brass: it was hollow, was filled with earth, probably to half its height, and the upper half was pierced so as to admit freely currents of fresh air, to supply the place of the rarefied that rose from the heated grate on the surface, and to aid in the total consumption of the victims which were offered there.

The Altar stood due east and west, and its four corners were surmounted with horns. To these horns those fled who took sanctuary (see the example of Joab); and some imagine that victims were bound to them, as it is written: "Bind the sacrifice with cords, even to the horns of the Altar."

But the best authorities translate this passage: "Bind the sacrifice with cords until it reaches the horns of the Altar." Below the horns were rings into which staves were inserted by which the Altar was borne in their journeys; but when the Tabernacle was set up and at rest, the smoke of the sacrifices which were consumed upon it rose incessantly night and day.

The Golden Altar

(*See Note I*).

Immediately behind the Vail which separated the Holy Place from the Court stood the Golden Altar, or, as it is also called, the Altar of Incense.

It was smaller than the Altar in the Court; was made of shittim-wood, overlaid within and without with fine gold; was surmounted by four horns and a golden crown, and underneath the horns were rings as in the brazen altar, and for the same purpose: so also, in the Golden Table and the Ark of the Covenant. On the Golden Altar holy incense was offered by the priests every morning and evening, and the smoke of the incense, like the smoke of the sacrifices in the Court, rose continually towards heaven.

No common fire was permitted to burn on this altar. Its fire was commanded to be brought from the outer altar. Nadab and Abihu transgressed this law when they offered the daily incense; but a still holier fire avenged their sin, for fire came out from the Lord (i.e. from the Mercy Seat in the Most Holy Place), and slew them.

Neither was this incense permitted to be offered by any Israelite who was not of the Aaronic family. Korah, although a Levite, and the princes who leagued with him, were destroyed because they heeded not this exclusion; and their censers, beaten into tablets, were kept as "a memorial unto the children of Israel, that no stranger, which is not of the seed of Aaron, come near to offer incense before the Lord; that he be not as Korah, and as his company." (Numbers 26:40)

Unfortunately, King Uzziah, a good and prosperous prince, neglected this prohibition and terrible example.

> "When he was strong,
> His heart was lifted up to his destruction:
> For he transgressed against the Lord his God,
> And went into the Temple of the Lord
> To burn incense upon the altar of incense.
> And Azariah the priest went in after him,
> And with him fourscore priests of the Lord,
> That were valiant men:
> And they withstood Uzziah the king,
> And said unto him,
> It appertained not unto thee, Uzziah,
> To burn incense unto the Lord,
> But to the priests the sons of Aaron,

That are consecrated to burn incense:
Go out of the Sanctuary;
For thou hast trespassed;
Neither shall it be for thine honor from the Lord God.
Then Uzziah was wroth,
And he had a censer in his hand to burn incense:
And while he was wroth with the priests,
The leprosy even rose up in his forehead
Before the priests in the house of the Lord,
From beside the incense altar.
And Azariah, the chief priest,
And all the priests, looked upon him,
And, behold, he was leprous in his forehead,
And they thrust him out from thence;
Yea, himself hasted also to go out,
Because the Lord had smitten him.
And Uzziah the king was a leper unto the day of his death,
And dwelt in a several house,
Being a leper." (2 Chronicles 26:16-21)

At this altar, in Herod's Temple, stood Zacharias, the father of John the Baptist, to burn incense while the people were praying without in the Court, when the angel Gabriel appeared to him.

The Golden Candlestick

(*See Note K*).

Further west, and nearer the Vail of the Most Holy, on the south side of the Holy Place, stood the Golden Candlestick.

As in the other exceptional case of the Laver, we have no description of the height, or the precise outlines of this sacred vessel; and it must ever remain an unsolved problem whether the seven lamps were all in a line or pyramidal, and whether the shaft and branches were sufficiently low to allow of the lamps being lighted without the aid of steps, or not.

The candlestick on the Arch of Titus was confessedly a representation of that in the second Temple, and may possibly have preserved the type of the Mosaic, although critics maintain that the base of the sculptured effigy is purely pagan, and that its branches only appear of Hebrew origin.

I presume that, if we had some definite knowledge of the style of Hebrew architecture, we should find no difficulty to determine, from the minute description of the ornaments of the Candlestick, both its height and precise conformation; but, at present, without even one authentic fragment to guide us, the task is hopeless.

Still, in reference to this sacred vessel, as in regard to all the other vessels, and the House of God itself, the description which remains is sufficient to enable us to decipher some of those grand lessons which they were intended to convey.

The general outlines of the Golden Candlestick seem to have been as follows:

1. Its golden shaft, according to Gesenius (*Thea, s. v. Jareck.*) and Maimonides, terminated downwards in three feet, or roots, and upwards in one of the seven branches on which the lamps were placed.

2. Six hollow branches, bent upwards in the form of a segment, rose laterally out of the central branch: and on the top of these seven branches, which Josephus says stood parallel to one another, but which others maintain to have been in the form of a pyramid, deep moveable lamps were placed, which were filled with oil, and lighted.

3. Three mystic ornaments, consisting of blossoms, fruit-buds, and lilies, were set in clusters on the seven branches—three clusters of three in the lateral branches, and four clusters of three in the center.

4. The general appearance, therefore, of the Candlestick seems to have been that of a tree with three roots, with stem or trunk, branches, foliage, blossoms, and buds, of which the burning lamps formed the splendid fruit.

The Golden Table

(*See Note L*).

On the north side of the Holy Place, over against the Candlestick, stood the Golden Table, Or the Table of Shewbread as it is also called. Its form and dimensions are carefully described.

It was made of wood, cased in gold, was "four-square," and had four feet. Josephus says the latter resembled those which the Dorians put to their bedsteads, which is indeed most unlikely, and the resemblance between Hebrew and Grecian art had probably no other foundation than the pitiful weakness of this writer to place his nation on the miserable level of heathen civilization. Like the Golden Altar, the Table had also a Golden Crown; or, according to Abarbanel's interpretation of the words,

> "Thou shalt make thereto a crown of gold round about . . .
> And thou shalt make a golden crown to the border thereof."

It had two crowns, one above and the other below the rim.

On this Table the twelve loaves of Shewbread were placed, which were renewed every Sabbath day, and eaten by the priests in the Holy place, or, as the Rabbins say, *intra vela*. On the bread they placed holy incense, and, if Philo may be trusted, salt also and wine.

Twenty cubits from the eastern extremity of the Holy Place hung the magnificent Vail of the Most Holy, embroidered with crimson, purple, blue, and with Cherubim.

Behind that Vail ventured none for the offering of prayer, or of blood, except the High Priest alone, once in the year. That highest division had neither natural light like the Court, nor artificial light like the Holy Place, but was illumined by a miraculous Cloud which appeared over the Ark of the Covenant.

Josephus relates that Pompey forced his way into the Holy Place of the second Temple, and into the Most Holy, but that he saw nothing in the latter, for the Ark of the Covenant had never been recovered since the fall of the first Temple; although Durandus strangely asserts that Titus had brought it to Rome, where it had been preserved to his day. Only a marble pedestal marked the place in the second Temple where the Ark had stood in the first, and in the Tabernacle; nor had it the Mercy Seat, or Cherubim, or the miraculous Cloud.

The Ark of the Covenant

(*See Note M*).

The Ark was a "four-square" chest of shittim-wood, overlaid within and without with pure gold. In it Moses laid the Tables of the Law, a pot of manna, and Aaron's rod that budded. Upon it lay

The Mercy Seat

The Mercy Seat was a massive lid of pure gold which squared exactly with the Ark; and at the two extremities of the Mercy Seat north and south, and of the same precious metal—nay, part of it—rose the two

Cherubims of Glory

with their faces turned toward each other, but inclined to the Mercy Seat, and overshadowing it with their outstretched wings.

The word Cherub has been derived from the Chaldee, in which language it means "Like a little child!' or from the Hebrew, where it signifies "Like the Lord, or Master." The other name, of Living Creatures, given to the Cherubim in the Scriptures, is said to denote beings in whom created life has reached its fullest and most glorious development (*See Note N*).

To me it seems that the Cherubim combine all these meanings, and symbolize those happiest of created beings who are at once like little children and like the Lord, and in whom life has reached the highest attainable point of intelligence, affection, and exuberant enjoyment.

The human form seems upon the whole to have predominated in the Cherubim. Thus, Ezekiel says expressly of the Cherubim which he saw in vision:

> "This was their appearance;
> They had the likeness of a man:" (Ezekiel 1:5)

and the Jewish writers speak of them as human beings—as male and female.

The Cherubim which Moses placed over the Ark cannot have had more than one face a-piece, though those of Ezekiel's vision had four; for it is said expressly; "Their faces shall look one to another: toward the Mercy Seat shall the faces of the Cherubim be." (Exodus 25:20) If, however, as for example the Hutchinsonians imagine, they had four faces on four sides each, like those seen by the river Chebar, they could not possibly have fulfilled this condition.

Their wings seem to have been two a-piece, like those of the two larger Cherubim which Solomon added. Thus, at least, it seems most natural to understand the words of the Lord to Moses:

> "And the Cherubim shall stretch forth their wings on high,
> Covering (overshadowing) the Mercy Seat with their wings." (Exodus 25:20)

It is true that in other parts of Holy Scripture the Cherubim differ from this description, but they follow a definite law of development on which I cannot enter at present, as its proper statement would require a separate essay. But after all, it affects not the great lesson I am anxious to point out in this volume, whether the wings of the Mosaic Cherubim were two, as I have stated, or more.

The Cloud of Glory

Between the Cherubim, over the Mercy Seat, rested the luminous, fiery Cloud, called the Shekinah. Holy Scripture speaks of it as follows:

> "The Lord said unto Moses,
> Speak unto Aaron thy brother,
> That he come not at all times into the Holy Place
> Within the Vail,
> Before the Mercy Seat, which is upon the Ark,
> That he die not:
> For I will appear in the cloud upon the Mercy Seat." (Leviticus 16:2)

This miraculous light remained there always, and hence that prayer: "O Thou that dwellest between the Cherubim, shine forth."

And here I close the sketch of the Holy Tabernacle and its Vessels; and proceed to point out some of the lessons which I believe it was intended to inculcate.

NOTE A

"And thou shalt make the court of the Tabernacle:
For the south side southward
There shall be hangings for the court
Of fine twined linen,
Of an hundred cubits long for one side:
And the twenty pillars thereof,
And their twenty sockets shall be of brass;
The hooks of the pillars,
And their fillets shall be of silver.
And likewise, for the north side in length,
There shall be hangings
Of an hundred cubits long,
And his twenty pillars,
And their twenty sockets of brass;
The hooks of the pillars and their fillets of silver.
All the pillars round about the court
Shall be filleted with silver;
Their hooks shall be of silver,
And their sockets of brass.
The length of the court
Shall be an hundred cubits,
And the breadth fifty everywhere,
And the height five cubits,

Of fine twined linen,
And their sockets of brass.
And for the breadth of the court,
On the west side,
Shall be hangings of fifty cubits:
Their pillars ten,
And their sockets ten.
And the breadth of the court,
On the east side eastward
Shall be fifty cubits.
The hangings of one side of the gate
Shall be fifteen cubits,
Their pillars three,
And their sockets three.
And on the other side
Shall be hangings fifteen cubits;
Their pillars three,
And their sockets three." (Exodus 27:9-15, 17, 18)

NOTE B

"And for the gate of the court
There shall be an hanging of twenty cubits,
Of blue, and purple, and scarlet, and fine twined linen,
Wrought with needlework:
And their pillars shall be four
And their sockets four." (Exodus 27:16)

NOTE C

"And thou shalt make boards for the Tabernacle
Of shittim-wood standing up.

Ten cubits shall be the length of a board,
And a cubit and a half shall be the breadth of one board.
Two tenons shall there be in one board,
Set in order one against another:
Thus, shalt thou make for all the boards of the Tabernacle.
And thou shalt make the boards for the Tabernacle
Twenty boards on the south side southward.
And thou shalt make forty sockets of silver,
Under the twenty boards:
Two sockets under one board for his two tenons,
And two sockets under another board for his two tenons.
And for the second side of the Tabernacle,
On the north side,
There shall be twenty boards;
And their forty sockets of silver;
Two sockets under one board,
And two sockets under another board.
And for the sides of the Tabernacle westward
Thou shalt make six boards.
And two boards shalt thou make,
For the corners of the Tabernacle,
In the two sides.
And they shall be coupled together beneath,
And they shall be coupled together above
The head of it unto one ring.
Thus, shall it be for them both;
They shall be for the two corners,
And they shall be eight boards,
And their sockets of silver, sixteen sockets;
Two sockets under one board,
And two sockets under another board.
And thou shalt make bars of shittim-wood;

Five for the boards of the one side of the Tabernacle,
And five bars for the boards of the other side of the Tabernacle,
And five bars for the boards of the side of the Tabernacle,
For the two sides westward
And the middle bar in the midst of the boards
Shall reach from end to end.
And thou shalt overlay the boards with gold,
And make their rings of gold,
For places for the bars:
And thou shalt overlay the bars with gold.
And thou shalt rear up the Tabernacle
According to the fashion thereof
Which was showed thee in the Mount." (Exodus 26:15-29)

NOTE D

"Moreover, thou shalt make the Tabernacle
With ten curtains
Of fine twined linen, and blue and purple, and scarlet
With cherubim of cunning work,
Shalt thou make them.
The length of one curtain
Shall be eight-and-twenty cubits,
And the breadth of one curtain four cubits:
And every one of the curtains shall have one measure.
The five curtains shall be coupled together one to another;
And other five curtains shall be coupled one to another.
And thou shalt make loops of blue,
Upon the edge of one curtain from the selvedge in the coupling;
And likewise shalt thou make in the uttermost
Edge of another curtain,
In the coupling of the second.

Fifty loops shalt thou make in the one curtain,
And fifty loops shalt thou make in the edge of the curtain,
That is in the coupling of the second;
That the loops may take hold one of another.
And thou shalt make fifty taches of gold,
And couple the curtains together with the taches:
And it shall be one Tabernacle.
And thou shalt make curtains of goat's hair,
To be a covering upon the Tabernacle:
Eleven curtains shalt thou make.
The length of one curtain shall be thirty cubits,
And the breadth of one curtain four cubits:
And the eleven curtains shall be all of one measure.
And thou shalt couple five curtains by themselves,
And six curtains by themselves,
And shall double the sixth curtain,
In the forefront of the Tabernacle.
And thou shalt make fifty loops,
On the edge of the one curtain that is outmost in the coupling,
And fifty loops on the edge of the curtain
Which coupleth the second.
And thou shalt make fifty taches of brass,
And put the taches into the loops,
And couple the tent together, that it may be one.
And the remnant that remained of the curtains of the tent,
The half curtain that remained,
Shall hang over the backside of the Tabernacle.
And a cubit on the one side,
And a cubit on the other side
Of that which remained in the length of the curtains of the tent,
It shall hang over the sides of the Tabernacle,
On this side and on that side, to cover it.

And thou shalt make a covering for the tent
Of rams' skins dyed red,
And a covering above of badgers' skins." (Exodus 26:1-14)

NOTE E

"And thou shalt make an hanging
For the door of the tent,
Of blue, and purple, and scarlet, and fine twined linen,
Wrought with needlework.
And thou shalt make for the hanging
Five pillars of shittim-wood,
And overlay them with gold,
And their hooks shall be of gold:
And thou shalt cast five sockets of brass for them." (Exodus 26:36-37)

NOTE F

"And thou shalt make a Vail
Of blue, and purple, and scarlet, and fine twined linen
Of cunning work: with cherubim shall it be made:
And thou shalt hang it upon four pillars of shittim-wood
Overlaid with gold:
Their hooks shall be of gold,
Upon the four sockets of silver.
And thou shalt hang up the Vail under the taches,
That thou mayest bring in thither within the Vail
The Ark of the Testimony:
And the Vail shall divide unto you
Between the Holy Place and the Most Holy." (Exodus 26:31-33)

NOTE G

"And the Lord spoke unto Moses, saying,
Thou shalt also make a Laver of brass,
And his foot also of brass,
To wash withal:
And thou shalt put it between the Tabernacle
Of the Congregation and the Altar,
And thou shalt put water therein.
For Aaron and his sons shall wash thereat
Their hands and their feet:
When they go into the Tabernacle of the Congregation,
They shall wash with water, that they die not;
Or when they come near the Altar to minister,
To burn offering made by fire unto the Lord;
So, they shall wash their hands and their feet,
That they die not;
And it shall be a. statute for ever to them,
Even to him and to his seed
Throughout them generations." (Exodus 30:17-22)

"And he made the Laver of brass,
And the foot of it of brass,
Of the looking-glasses of the women assembling,
Which assembled at the door of the
Tabernacle of the Congregation." (Exodus 38:8)

NOTE H

"And thou shalt make an Altar of shittim-wood,
Five cubits long, and five cubits broad;
The Altar shall be four-square:
And the height thereof shall be three cubits.

And thou shalt make the horns of it
Upon the four corners thereof:
His horns shall be of the same:
And thou shalt overlay it with brass.
And thou shalt make his pans to receive his ashes
And his shovels and his basons,
And his flesh hooks, and his fire pans:
All the vessels thereof thou shalt make of brass.
And thou shalt make for it a grate of network of brass;
And upon the net thou shalt make four brazen rings
In the four corners thereof.
And thou shalt put it under the compass of the Altar beneath,
That the net may be even to the midst of the Altar.
And thou shalt make staves for the Altar,
Staves of shittim-wood,
And overlay them with brass.
And the staves shall be put into the rings,
And the staves shall be upon the two sides of the Altar to bear it.
Hollow with boards shalt thou make it:
As it was showed thee in the Mount,
So, shall they make it." (Exodus 37:1-8)

"And thou shalt anoint the Altar of the Burnt offering
And all his vessels,
And sanctify the Altar,
And it shall be an Altar most holy." (Exodus 40:10)

"And Moses took the anointing oil,
And anointed the Tabernacle and all that was therein,
And sanctified them.
And he sprinkled thereof upon the Altar seven times,
And anointed the Altar and all the vessels,
Both the Laver and his foot, to sanctify them." (Leviticus 8:10-11)

NOTE I

"And thou shalt make an altar to burn incense:
Of shittim-wood shalt thou make it.
A cubit shall be the length thereof,
And a cubit the breadth thereof;
Four-square shall it be:
And two cubits shall be the height thereof:
The horns thereof shall be of the same.
And thou shalt overlay it with pure gold,
The top thereof, and the sides thereof round about,
And the horns thereof;
And thou shalt make unto it's a crown of gold round about.
And two golden rings shalt thou make to it
Under the crown of it, by the two corners thereof,
Upon the two sides of it shalt thou make it;
And they shall be for places for the staves to bear it withal.
And thou shalt make the staves of shittim-wood,
And overlay them with gold.
And thou shalt put it before the Vail
That is by the Ark of the Testimony,
Before the mercy seat that is over the Testimony,
Where I will meet with thee.
And Aaron shall burn thereon sweet incense, every morning;
When he dresseth the lamps,
He shall burn incense upon it.
And when Aaron lighteth the lamps at even,
He shall burn incense upon it,
A perpetual incense before the Lord,
Throughout your generations.
Ye shall offer no strange incense thereon,
Nor burnt sacrifice, nor meat offering;

Neither shall ye pour drink offering thereon.
And Aaron shall make an atonement
Upon the horns of it once in a year,
With the blood of the sin offering of atonements;
Once in the year shall he make atonement upon it
Throughout your generations;
It is most holy unto the Lord." (Exodus 30:1-10)

NOTE K

"And thou shalt make a candlestick of pure gold:
Of beaten work shall the candlestick be made;
His shaft, and his branches,
His bowls, his knops, and his flowers, shall be of the same.
And six branches shall come out of the sides of it;
Three branches of the candlestick out of the one side,
And three branches of the candlestick out of the other side:
Three bowls made like unto almonds,
With a knop and a flower in one branch,
And three bowls made like almonds in the other branch,
With a knop and a flower:
So, in the six branches that come out of the candlestick.
And in the candlestick shall be four bowls;
Made like unto almonds, with their knops and their flowers.
And there shall be a knop under two branches of the same,
And a knop under two branches of the same,
And a knop under two branches of the same,
According to the six branches
That proceed out of the candlestick.
Their knops and their branches shall be of the same:
All it shall be one beaten work of pure gold.
And thou shalt make the seven lamps thereof:

And they shall light the lamps thereof,
That they may give light over against it.
And the tongs thereof, and the snuff dishes thereof,
Shall be of pure gold.
Of a talent of pure gold shall he make it,
With all these vessels.
And look that thou make them after their pattern,
Which was showed thee in the mount." (Exodus 25:31-40)
"And thou shalt command the children of Israel,
That they bring thee pure olive oil beaten for the light,
To cause the lamp to burn always.
In the Tabernacle of the congregation without the Vail,
Which is before the Testimony,
Aaron and his sons shall order it
From evening till morning before the Lord:
It shall be a statute forever unto their generations
On behalf of the children of Israel." (Exodus 27:20-21)

The lamps were trimmed afresh every morning, also, at the offering of incense:

"And Aaron shall burn thereon [on the golden altar]
Sweet incense every morning:
When he dresseth the lamps, he shall burn incense
Upon incense upon it." (Exodus 30:7)
"He shall order the lamps upon the pure candlestick,
Before the Lord continually." (Leviticus 24:4)

NOTE L

"Thou shalt also make a Table of shittim-wood:
Two cubits shall be the length thereof,

And a. cubit the breadth thereof,
And a cubit and a half the height thereof.
And thou shalt overlay it with pure gold,
And make thereto a crown of gold round about.
And thou shalt make unto it a border
Of a hand breadth round about,
And thou shalt make a golden crown
To the border thereof round about.
And thou shalt make for it four rings of gold,
And put the rings in the four corners,
That are on the four feet thereof.
Over against the border shall the rings be,
For places of the staves to bear the Table.
And thou shalt make the staves of shittim-wood,
Aand overlay them with gold,
That the Table may be borne with them.
And thou shalt make the dishes thereof,
And spoons thereof,
And covers thereof,
And bowls thereof to cover withal:
Of pure gold shalt thou make them.
And thou shalt set upon the Table shewbread before me always."
(Exodus 25:23, 30)

"And thou shalt take fine flour and bake twelve cakes thereof:
Two tenth deals shall be in one cake.
And thou shalt set them in two rows, six on a row,
Upon the pure Table before the Lord.
Every Sabbath he shall set it in order before the Lord continually,
Being taken from the children of Israel
By an everlasting covenant.
And it shall be Aaron's and his sons;
And they shall eat it in the Holy Place:

For it is most holy unto him
Of the offerings of the Lord made by fire
By a perpetual statute." (Leviticus 24:5-9)

NOTE M

"And they shall make an Ark of shittim-wood:
Two cubits and a half shall be the length thereof,
And a cubit and a half the breadth thereof,
And a cubit and a half the height thereof.
And thou shalt overlay it with pure gold,
Within and without shalt thou overlay it,
And shalt make upon it a crown of gold round about.
And thou shalt cast four rings of gold for it,
And put them in the four corners thereof;
And two rings shall be in the one side of it,
And two rings in the other side of it.
And thou shalt make staves of shittim-wood,
And overlay them with gold.
And thou shalt put the staves into the rings
By the sides of the Ark,
That the Ark may be home with them.
The staves shall be in the rings of the Ark:
They shall not be taken from it.
And thou shalt put into the Ark
The testimony which I shall give thee.
And thou shalt make a mercy seat of pure gold:
Two cubits and a half shall be the length thereof,
And a cubit and a half the breadth thereof.
And thou shalt make two cherubim of gold,
Of beaten work shalt thou make them,
In the two ends of the mercy seat.

And make one cherub on the one end,
And the other cherub on the other end:
Even of the mercy seat shall ye make the cherubim
On the two ends thereof.
And the cherubim shall stretch forth their wings on high,
Covering the mercy seat with their wings,
And their faces shall look one to another:
Toward the mercy seat shall the faces of the cherubim be.
And thou shalt put the mercy seat above upon the Ark;
And in the Ark, thou shalt put the testimony
That I shall give thee.
And there will I meet with thee,
And I will commune with thee from above the mercy seat,
Between the two cherubim which are upon
The Ark of the Testimony,
Of all things which I will give thee
In commandment unto the children of Israel." (Exod. 25:11—22)

NOTE N

There are few subjects on which a more extraordinary diversity of opinion exists than on the meaning of the cherubim.

I shall adduce a few of these opinions, in order to impress the reader with the importance of hold ing fast by the interpretation which the Scriptures give of this symbol.

Philo regarded the cherubim as representing the universe, and reflecting God's wisdom, knowledge, justice, and mercy. Very similar to this is the view of Baehr.

The Cabalists spoke of them as the chieftains of the four worlds—the world of pure emanations; the world of spirits unembodied and incapable of acting on matter; the world of spirits embodied (angels); and of the lower world of matter. They regarded also the vision in which Ezekiel saw them, and which, on account of the wheels appearing in it, they called Mercabah, or the Chariot—as the index of the deepest mysteries of God that are revealed to man.

> "In Cabala Mercavae summa contineri, quae concipi possunt, et profoundissima mysteria, vulgarique Philosopho vix credibilia." (Rosenroth. Cab. Den. Vis. Ezech. Expos. i. Postul. l.)

And so, the Christian Mystics. The Hutchinsonians regarded the cherubim as figures of the Holy Trinity.

They say (see Parkhurst, Gr. Lex. s.v. Cherubim):

> "That the cherubic figures were emblems or representatives of something beyond themselves is, I think, agreed by all, both Jews and Christians; but the question is, of what they were emblematical. To which I answer in a word: Those in the Holy of Holies [which Holy of Holies, of the Tabernacle or Temple, he does not say] were emblematical of the ever-blessed Trinity, in covenant to redeem man, by uniting the human nature to the Second Person, which union was signified by the union of the faces of the lion and of the man in the cherubic exhibition." (Ezekiel 1:10, comp. Ezekiel 12:18-19)

> "The cherubim in the Holy of Holies were certainly intended to represent some beings in heaven; because St. Paul has expressly and infallibly determined that the Holy of Holies was a figure or type of heaven, even of that heaven where is the peculiar residence of God (Hebrews 9:24); and therefore, these cherubim represented either the ever-blessed Trinity, with the man taken into the essence, or created spiritual angels."

This is very inconclusive: for granting that the cherubim represent some beings in heaven, are there no other beings there besides the most blessed Trinity and the holy angels? Are not the spirits of just men made perfect there also?

Another ancient Jewish tradition says (B. Uzi Elin Isa. vi. 3): "The two cherubim in the Tabernacle were male and female . . . to signify, says Abarbanel, in his Excursus on Exodus, that both sexes in Israel should study the law . . ." or to show, says another commentator, that God loves his Church as a man loves his wife. Aben Ezra thinks them winged human beings. Sin, they say, has deprived man of his wings, which are to be restored in the consummation; and they speak of the shoulder, or so scapula, as ala ossification, an ossified wing.

Other Jewish commentators regard the four cherubim as emblematical of the four camps of Israel, on whose standards the four cherubic signs were said to have been emblazoned. So also, Lowth; so also, Bengal on the Apocalypse. He says: "According to the testimony of the ancient Hebrews, the people had four banners in their four camps, and that of Judah, in the east, bore the lion; Ephraim, in the west, the bull (calf); Reuben, in the south, a man; and Dan, in the north, a flying eagle. . . . . And," he adds, "the four cherubim, and the first four seals in the Revelation, are referred, with good reason, to the four quarters of the globe; since Israel is scattered into all the world . . . Some believe them to be the holy men who wrote the Gospels; but the position of an Evangelist is not so high." See Ephesians 4:11."

Irenaeus and St. Augustine believed the four cherubim of the Apocalypse to be emblematical of the four Evangelists and their Gospels. But Irenaeus seemed uncertain, and compares them also to the four elements, the four quarters of the world, and the four universal covenants.

Justin Martyr spoke of them as symbolical of Nebuchadnezzar in his madness, when he ate grass like an ox, his hair resembled a lion's mane, and his hands had grown like eagles' talons. In such great diversity of opinion, it is manifestly clear that our only safe guide in search of the meaning of the cherubim is Holy Scripture.

2

Proof from Scripture

Proof from Scripture that the Holy Tabernacle was a Type or Shadow of the Church of God, and of Her Local Habitation

The first and most obvious end for which the Tabernacle was erected was to serve as a place for solemn worship. Thus it is said in the Psalms:

> "As for me, I will come into Thy house
> In the multitude of Thy mercy,
> I will worship toward thy holy Temple." (Psalm 5:7)

But the circumstance that much of that worship consisted in acts full of solemn mystery; of the transfer of sin, by imposition of hands, from the soul of the sinner to the head of an innocent victim; of the slaying of countless sacrifices, sometimes by tens of thousands in one day (*According to Josephus, they sacrificed two hundred and and fifty-six thousand and five hundred Paschal Lambs in one day—Wars, vi. 9, 3. And Bochart, Hieroz. t. l, lib. ii. cap. 50, p. 575, points, in confirmation of this, to the fact that at the Consecration of the Temple, Solomon offered two hundred and twenty thousand oxen, and one hundred and twenty thousand sheep; to which the people added sacrifices "which could not be told nor numbered for multitude." 2 Chronicles 5:6.*); of strange mystic sprinkling of the blood, or, as Holy Scripture calls it, the life of the victims towards the Divine presence; of ceaseless and costly burnings on the holy altar; of taking blood, and fire, and incense into the Holy Place behind the Vail, whither no eye could follow, nor dared on pain of death; of still rarer and more mysterious acts that happened at longer intervals—acts which only their highest religious functionary was allowed to perform, and for which he prepared himself with appalling solemnity; all this must have forced on more thoughtful minds the conviction that more was intended by that house of God than a mere place of worship, and hence the saints of the ancient economy uttered such prayers as these,

> "Open Thou mine eyes,
> That I may behold wondrous things out of Thy law!" (Psalm 119:18)

> "One thing have I desired of the Lord,
> That will I seek after:
> That I may dwell in the house of the Lord all the days of my life,
> To behold the beauty of the Lord, and to *inquire* in His Temple!"
> (Psalm 27:4)

But the New Testament places this deeper meaning beyond mere inference, and assumes it as known and believed in the Church of Israel. I shall venture to state this point in the following propositions:

First Proposition

The Tabernacle of Moses was a figure of the true Tabernacle.

> "Christ is not entered into the Holy Places
> Made with hands,
> Which are *the figures*..." (Hebrews 9:24)

("Holy Places," stands for the whole Tabernacle—Court, Holy Place, and Most Holy, in Exodus 36:1, Leviticus 16:11 and 26:2, Numbers 4:15,

twice; 19:20, &c. See LXX. ed. Tischendorf; and it is an obvious canon of interpretation that we should explain words in the New Testament according to their meaning in the Old. The term "figures" refers to copy, image, effigy, or likeness, corresponding to the original types shown to Moses in the Mount, Hebrews 8:5.—Stuart, l. c. "The Sacraments were often designated by this epithet, as representing to us Christ." Alford, ibid. ... denoting the resemblance relative to Christ both in His Mediatorial High-Priestly capacity, and as Lord in Heaven." Bloomfield, ibid) of the true [Tabernacle]." Hebrews 9:24)

Second Proposition

The true Tabernacle is the heavenly Sanctuary, and the two expressions, the "true Tabernacle" and the "heavenly Sanctuary" are synonymous. "Now of the things which we have spoken,

> *This is the sum:*
> *We have such an High Priest*
> *Who is set on My right hand*
> *Of the throne*
> *Of My majesty in the heavens,*
> *A Minister of fire sanctuary,*
> And of the true Tabernacle, and
> Which the Lord pitched, And not man." (Hebrews 8:1)

If, as Alford says in the preceding note, the earthly Tabernacle stood in the same relation to the true as the elements in the Holy Eucharist to Christ, then is the true Tabernacle not merely a transient vision which appeared to Moses in the Mount, but some exalted reality. It is evidently the sphere of the Savior's ministry, the testimony of all commentators to which I have access at present, concurs in this view.

"The heavenly things, being invisible and not grossly material, are true; but earthly things, because they are merely visible and grossly material exemplars, are said to be untrue." (Origen in Cant. De Wette, l. c., and Hebrews 9:24, call the true Tabernacle the heavenly sanctuary.)

"The true Tabernacle," says Delitsch, quoted by Alford, "is the heavenly Jerusalem, the worship-place of blessed spirits, and of those men who have been rapt in vision thither (Isaiah 6), . . . the place where God's visible presence . . . is manifested to His creatures, angelic and human."

"Minister of the Sanctuary . . . the high-priest of the Temple above. The true Tabernacle means that which is spiritual, immutable, and eternal in the heavens, and which therefore is called true, or real, in distinction from the earthly Tabernacle, which was made by the hands of men, and was of materials earthly and perishable. The Tabernacle in the heavens is the substance, that on earth the image or type. Hence the former is, by way of distinction, is real, or that which permanently exists." (Stuart, l. c.)

"The true Tabernacle, the archetypal, only true, as so often in the book of John, and in one passage in Luke, 16:11." (Alford, l. c.)

"It is the entrance of Christ into the heavenly Sanctuary, of which the writer is here speaking. That Christ performs the office of priest in the heavenly sanctuary, the writer has already intimated several times." (Stuart, 1. c.)

Third Proposition

But the heavenly Sanctuary is also called the House of God; and the two expressions, the "true Tabernacle" and the "House of God" are synonymous, when it is said:

> "Having therefore, brethren,
> Boldness to enter
> Into the Holiest
> By the blood of Jesus,
> By a new and living way,
> Which He hath consecrated for us,
> Through the Vail,
> That is to say, His Flesh;
> And having an High Priest
> Over the house of God
> Let us draw near
> With a true heart..." (Hebrews 10:19-22)

(*See note on the signification of the expression "into the Holiest" on p. 641, "The heavenly Sanctuary."-De Wette, l. c. Regarding the expression the house of God, "Not the people or family of God, nor the faithful, but ... the heavenly Sanctuary." De Wette, Theopl. 2; Bhm. Kuin. Thol. Bleek. "The spiritual house of God;" Stuart, ibid. — "meaning, it would seem, the true Sanctuary, heaven ... Bloomfield, ibid.*)

If, then, the Mosaic Tabernacle was a type of the true Tabernacle, and the true Tabernacle synonymous with the House of God, it follows that the Tabernacle was a type of the House of God.

We may arrive at the same conclusion by a shorter way. The Tabernacle was the dwelling of God, as it is written:

> "Let them make Me a sanctuary,
> That I may dwell among them." (Exodus 25:8)

But dwelling and house are synonymous; and the various Hebrew terms by which the Tabernacle is designated in the Scriptures were therefore rendered by the LXX with *oikos*, or house. If, then, the Mosaic Tabernacle may be rendered the earthly house of God, the true Tabernacle which it foreshadowed may also be rendered the true, i. e. [see note at the end of the chapter) the spiritual and immutable house of God, *q. e. d.*

Nor is it difficult to ascertain the exact meaning of this familiar Scriptural expression. It occurs in the two meanings, viz.: —

> 1st Of a local sphere in which God dwells; and
> 2nd. Of a community of men with whom He dwells.

In the first sense the expression, House of God, and the similar expressions, the House of the Lord, the Habitation or Dwelling place of God, occur in too great a number of passages to be quoted here. A few instances will suffice. Thus, the patriarch Jacob says of the place where he had seen God in vision,

> "Surely, the Lord is in this place
> And I knew it not . . .
> How dreadful is this place!
> This is none other than the House of God." (Genesis 28:16-17)

Moses prays,

> "Look down from Thy holy habitation from Heaven,
> And bless Thy people Israel . . ." (Deuteronomy 26:15)

In 2 Chronicles 30:27, it is said:

> "The priests . . . arose and blessed the people:
> And their voice was heard,
> And their prayer came up to His Holy Dwelling-place,
> Even unto Heaven."

Isaiah cries—

> "Look down from Heaven,
> And behold from the Habitation of Thy
> Holiness and of Thy Glory." (Isaiah 63:15)

Zachariah wrote:

> "Be silent, O all flesh, before the Lord,
> For He is raised up out of His Holy Habitation."
> (Zechariah 2:13)

In all these instances God's abode is distinctly asserted to be a Place; and our blessed Lord also speaks of the House of God as a local Habitation, when He says,

> "In my Father's House are many mansions:
> If it were not so I would have told you.
> I go to prepare a Place for you.
> And if I go and prepare a Place for you,
> I will come again, and receive you unto myself,
> That *where* I am, there ye may be also.
> And *whither* I go ye know." (John 14:2-4)

But in the second meaning the same expressions occur in such passages as the following:

> "Know ye not that ye are the Temple of God,
> And that the Spirit of God dwelleth in you?"
> (1 Corinthians 3:16)

> "We are Christ's House,
> If we hold fast the confidence
> And the rejoicing of the hope firm unto the end." (Hebrews 3:6)

> "Judgment must begin at the House of God." (1 Peter 4:17)

> "These things I write unto thee, that thou mayest know
> How thou oughest to behave thyself in the House of God,
> Which is the Church of the living God." (1 Timothy 3:14-15)

> "Ye are built upon the foundation of the Apostles and Prophets,
> Jesus Christ Himself being the Chief Cornerstone;
> In whom all the building fitly framed together
> Groweth into a holy Temple in the Lord
> In whom ye also are builded together
> For a Habitation of God through the Spirit." (Ephesians 2:20-23)

That the Tabernacle pointed to God's Habitation in this last sense is a conclusion supported by the concurrent testimony of all ages.

"From the days of Origen," says Tholuck, "to the present day, the Holy of Holies has been regarded as a type of the Church triumphant, and the Holy Place as the Type of the Church militant." (Thol. in Heb. vol. II. p. 21. Engl. Transl)

But I maintain, and hope to show satisfactorily, that the Tabernacle was a type of God's House in both acceptations of the term, viz.:

1. A type of the Community with whom God dwells; and

2. A type of the Local Sphere in which God dwells with this Community, or which this God-inhabited Community itself inhabits.

To this task I now address myself.

3

Progression of Glory

The Tabernacle, a Type of the House of God in the Sense of a Community

On examination, you will perceive a careful and systematic progress of glory marking the Holy Tabernacle in such manner that the Holy Place transcends the Court, and the Most Holy the Holy Place.

This feature is remarkable for its unmistakable design, and the simplicity and beauty with which this design is executed; nor seems it a small evidence of the verbal inspiration of this portion of the Bible, that if in any instance we substitute gold where silver is mentioned, or silver for brass, the solution of the symbolical enigma embodied in the Tabernacle is hopeless; but leave the words as they stand, and all is clear and most significant.

The Metals of the Tabernacle

Moses, as I have shown, was commanded to lay the foundations of the Court in brass, but those of the Holy Place in silver. The pillars of the Court were commanded to be made of wood with fillets (LXX, krikoi=rings) of silver; but the pillars composing the walls of the Holy Place were of wood, covered and crested with fine gold. Some have imagined that the less precious metals were used on account of the poverty of the people; but the abundance of gold in antiquity was prodigious, and seems to have been fairly shared by the Hebrews, who gave their treasures cheerfully and freely when the Tabernacle was erected.

The only sensible ground for the employment of various metals in the Tabernacle was evidently this—that, in unison and harmony with the rest of this mystic structure, they might convey the important lesson of gradation and progress. Nor is this the only place in Scripture where various metals are employed to indicate a gradation of glory.

Thus, e.g., Nebuchadnezzar sees in vision an image

> "Whose brightness was excellent,
> Whose head was of gold,
> His breast and his arms of silver,
> His belly and his thighs of brass,
> His legs of iron, his feet part of iron, and part of clay."
> (Daniel 2:31-33)

And the Prophet Daniel was divinely instructed to interpret the various metals, of various degrees of regal splendor, in five successive world empires declining from empire to empire precisely as the metals which foreshadowed them deteriorated from gold to silver, from silver to brass, from brass to iron, from iron to iron mingled with clay, and reaching the period of utter extinction when at last even the basest of these metals is destroyed.

Nor is it at all to be overlooked as though it were accidental, that the world's glory commences in this metaphorical image of Nebuchadnezzar with fine gold, and terminates in a confusion of iron and clay, while the Church's metaphor now before us begins with brass, but terminates in finest gold.

And the allocation of the various metals in the structure of the Holy Tabernacle utters a lesson so clear and beautiful as to leave no doubt of God's design in the arrangement. For the fact that the Court sprang from a foundation of brass, and attained only at its climax to a silver ring or fillet, while the Holy Place rose from massive foundations of silver, but attained to fine gold in stem and crest, declared in language as plain as can be uttered by metaphor, that the highest glory of what the Court foreshadowed was inferior to the lowest of that which was typified by the Holy Place.

The Hangings of the Tabernacle

But again—the Hangings of the Court, excepting the Vail of the Gate, were of fine linen simply; the Hangings of the Holy Place, on its ceiling and three sides, were of fine white linen richly embroidered with crimson, purple, and blue, and the forms of Cherubim. On the eastern extremity only—that is, at the entrance from the Court—there was a Vail like that in the Court, as if to declare that at the threshold of this Division, where also the five pillars stood in brazen sockets, there lingered some traces of the imperfections of the lower section, but traces which disappeared as you advanced.

The Vessels of the Tabernacle

And again—the Vessels of the Court were of imperishable wood and brass; but the Vessels of the Holy Place were of wood and fine gold.

Differences in Sacrifices

In the Court, victims were slain and consumed; in the Holy Place there was no death, and only part of the blood shed without was offered within this higher section: and whereas the light of the Court was the light of nature, with its alternations of day and night, though miraculously subdued by the overshadowing Cloud in the daytime, and relieved at night by its fiery splendor, the Holy Place excluded alike the darkness and the light of Nature, except as they crept faintly round its entrance—for this higher division was curtained in and vailed, and in it the Seven Golden Lamps shed their perpetual radiance.

On this wise rose the symbolical Glory of the Holy Place above that of the Court. And the Most Holy transcended the Holy Place as strikingly.

The foundations of the latter were, as we have seen, laid in silver, and the five pillars at its entrance stood in brass, but the foundations of the Most Holy were exclusively of silver; the Vail at the entrance of the Holy Place was like the Vail of the Court gate, and the girdle of the common priest; one, therefore, of the four sides of the Holy Place, when seen from within, was inferior to the rest, and like the Court; but the four walls of the Most Holy were alike glorious; and only in the highest section of the Temple did the Cherubim attain their greatest magnificence; for whilst they appeared merely in the embroidery of the Holy Place, they here stood forth sculptured in massive gold, and were called by Inspiration the Cherubim of Glory by way of eminence. And here, too, stood the Ark, that symbolical Throne of God, on which His visible Presence abode perpetually.

> "Here it was that the Shekinah, or Divine Presence, rested, both in the Tabernacle and the Temple, and was visibly seen in the appearance of a Cloud over it; and from hence the Divine Oracles were given out by an audible voice as often as God was consulted on behalf of His people. And hence it is that God is said in Scripture to dwell between the Cherubim on the Mercy Seat, because there was the seat or throne of the visible appearance of His Glory among them. And for this reason, the High Priest appeared before this Mercy Seat once every year on the great Day of Expiation, at which time he was to make his nearest approach to the Divine Presence; to mediate, and make

atonement for the whole people of Israel. The Ark of the Covenant was, as it were, the Center of worship to all those of that nation who served God according to the Levitical Law. And not only in the Temple, when they came thither to worship, but everywhere else in their dispersion throughout the whole world; whenever they prayed they turned their faces towards the place where the Ark stood, and directed all their devotions that way. Whence the author of the book of 'Cosri' justly says, that "the Ark, with the Mercy Seat and Cherubim, were the foundation, root, heart, and marrow of the whole Temple, and all the Levitical worship therein performed." (Hook's *Church Dict., s. v. Ark of the Cov.*)

Lighting in the Tabernacle

But once more. Whereas the Holy Place was lighted by those Seven Lamps of fire whose brightness depended on the obedience and vigilance of man—viz., of the priests who were commanded to tend them—the light of the Most Holy was not subject to such contingencies; for it proceeded from that miraculous fiery Cloud which rested on the Mercy Seat. It has therefore been justly said that, "as in the Most Holy the Shekinah, so in the Apocalypse God and the Lamb are said to be the light of the Heavenly Jerusalem, of which the Most Holy is the type."

Thus, did each successive section of the symbolical structure transcend the former in magnificence and glory. And if we turn from the shadow to the reality, we can scarcely fail to discover why the prototype demanded this division and progress. At the period of the erection of the Tabernacle the Church had just entered into her first economy—viz., the Mosaic, or the dispensation of the Law; and two others, then in the distant future, were destined to succeed it— viz., the dispensation of the Gospel, and the Status Gloria. Hence the necessity of the triple division of the Tabernacle.

But what, after all, are these dispensations of the Church but stages of development whose glory widens and deepens wonderfully as they succeed each other in her Heaven-appointed course?

Contrasted with the surrounding Paganism, yea, intrinsically, too, the first dispensation was full of spiritual splendor.

Out of the fast sinking nations of remote antiquity God called the Church of Israel as the depositary of His truth, and its destined restorer to mankind.

For this purpose He insulated her by a system of difficult laws, with fearful effect—enduring to this hour, after the lapse of more than thirty centuries—and by the many terrible judgments on her when she attempted to break through that insulation, and on other nations when they seriously interfered with it.

And when the belief in One Eternal God had "faded from the tablets of living opinion " and been superseded by the deification of nature; when the glories of creation were construed universally as a purely animal process, and worship had assumed forms so atrocious and obscene as to evoke the bitter complaint,

> "Every abomination under heaven
> Which the Lord hateth
> Have they done unto their gods;" (Deuteronomy 12:31);

when their very religion had sapped the foundations of physical being, and the soil beneath their feet grew restless, so that nothing remained but the destruction of whole nations among whom the defection had grown foulest even the extermination of everything that breathed, the precipitous heights and rugged glens of Judaea stood out amidst the gloom and darkness of the heathen world, a high-fenced and impregnable fortress of light and purity.

"Defile ye not yourselves in any of these things:
For in all these things the nations are defiled
Which I cast out before you:
And the land is defiled:
Therefore, I do visit the iniquity thereof upon it,
And the land itself vomiteth out her inhabitants."
(Leviticus 18:24-25)

Their ritual, regulating as it did every act of daily life, matured the consciousness of God's sovereign rule; their incessant cleansings deepened their knowledge of the defilement and peril of sin; their sacrifices fixed their minds on the coming Redeemer; and their prophetic holy seasons, cheered by song and festivity, kindled high hopes of coming perfect rest.

Dim, when compared with the brighter knowledge of the future, characteristic of our dispensation, were their anticipations of that rest and happiness—dim even to the practiced eye of the Prophets, for:

"They searched what,
And what manner of time
The Spirit of Christ which was in them did signify,
When it testified beforehand of the suffering of Christ,
And the glory that should follow." (1 Peter 1:11)

But although many members of the Church, like many nominal members of the Christian Church, were worthless, yet many were faithful; for it is written

"Israel was Holiness to the Lord." (Jeremiah 2:3)

There were even then men and women amongst them "of whom the world was not worthy;" whose deep faith, the apostle Paul says, stands forth as a witness to all time; thousands who, even in the deepening moral gloom of their closing polity, waited for the Consolation of Israel, and needed but the simple preaching of the Apostles to transform them into the heralds and martyrs of the Cross.

Yet the glory of that economy was but relative.

So, reasons Paul, when contrasting the Jewish and Christian Dispensations: he says,

> "If the ministry of Death,
> Written and engrave in stones, was glorious . . .
> How shall not the ministration of the Spirit
> Be rather glorious?
> For even that which was made glorious
> Had no glory in this respect,
> By reason of the glory that excellent." (2 Corinthians 3:7-10)

The advent of God in the flesh, His human sympathies, His teaching, His Cross and Passion, His glorious Resurrection and Ascension, and the coming of the Holy Ghost, have wondrously clarified the faith of the Church, and enlarged her vista of hope.

Still, even this 'higher dispensation is but relatively, not absolutely glorious, and destined to be eclipsed and forgotten in the future.

The Church is still divided—divided in more senses than one. Our Lord's prayer, that all the members of His Church should be one— one in sentiment and contiguity—is to all seeming far from its fulfilment. Long has His Church been distracted by incurable errors more or less grave, and inconquerable jealousies more or less embittered. Her outward unity is broken, and the host of God is marshalled in hostile factions. And what this side of the invisible world we, the Church's individual members, rightly hold most dear, is often mysteriously torn from us by the remorseless hand of death.

The spirits of our departed, they say, visit us in our holier moods! Yet is this cold mockery and miserable comfort. Yes, their memories come often, yet even these not always as a balm; but the loved spirits themselves seem far away—out of call in the seasons of perplexity, of desolation, and of mortal danger.

And as to our subjective state, are not God's saints constrained to this very hour to confess,

> "We see through a glass darkly:" (1 Corinthians 13:12)
> "The flesh lusted against the Spirit,
> And the Spirit against the flesh:
> And these are contrary the one to the other:
> So that we cannot do the things that we would." (Galatians 5:17)

We are still compelled to meet our foes unseen, and manifold are their advantages, and manifold our sore perplexities and defeats; the Savior, too, still remains invisible, and so is His Holy Spirit within the heart; and His best servants have sometimes wondered whether He has forsaken them. What marvel that even His saints grow weary, and the bitter cry is heard,

> "How long, O Lord, holy and true?" (Revelation 6:10)

Surely, our present condition is very far from absolute perfection. But a better state of things is promised, and may be imminent. The trump of God may even now be rising to the archangel's lip, at whose loud blast every shade and trace of sorrow and of sin shall flee away.

There is, therefore, a positive and strongly marked progression of glory in the Church's three dispensations which her type and similitude, if it is to be exact, must of necessity exhibit.

JERUSALEM THE GOLDEN

Nor is it easy to conceive of a more beautiful and striking symbolism than that by which the three sections of the Tabernacle achieve this end.

NOTE

"The immeasurable wealth in precious metals, but chiefly in gold, found, both in the remotest antiquity and in later periods, in the interior of Asia, must strike every student of Asiatic history, and is too well authenticated to leave room for reasonable doubt . . . The Ghaznavid and Mongols found, during their incursions in India, incalculable treasures, and were often obliged to throw away all their silver on account of the abundance of gold. . . Mahmud took from a single temple 700,000 gold coins, golden vessels weighing 28,000 pounds . . . and bars of gold weighing 1600 pounds . . . At Guzerat be robbed a temple of 56 columns of massive gold set with precious stones, and of a chain of gold weighing 1800 pounds. In 1290, Malik Allah took at Deogir, then the capital of Ramadeva, 15,000 pounds weight of gold, 175 pounds weight of pearls, and 50 pounds weight of precious stones. In 1306, the loot of Kafur, taken from Indian temples, amounted to 100 million sterling in gold, besides pearls and precious stones, and was taken away by 312 elephants and 20,000 horses. . . The wealth of Babylonia and Assyria appears to have been equally great."

"The Assyrian king Sardanapalus, when Nineveh was besieged, erected a pile on which he commanded his riches to be consumed, to prevent their falling into the hands of his enemies. Among his treasures were 150 bedsteads of gold, 150 golden tables, a million pounds weight in gold—although he had previously given 3000 hundredweight of gold to his sons. . . In the temple of Bel at Babylon there were in a lower chamber a statue of Bel, a throne and table weighing 800 talents; in the court an altar, and a statue of gold weighing 40 talents. On the pinnacle of the temple stood three statues of Jupiter (Bel), Juno, and Rhea, weighing 2800 talents... So also, in Persia."

"When Alexander entered Ecbatana, there were 120,000 hundred-weight of gold in its treasury; and the columns, halls, and courts were covered with gold and silver plates, and the roof was of silver... In Persepolis he is said to have found 120,000 talents of gold... The booty of Cyrus consisted of 34,000 pounds weight of gold, 500,000 hundred-weight of silver, besides a vast number of golden vessels, among which was the golden vase of Semiramis, which weighed 15 hundredweight..." (Baehr, *Symbol. d. Mos. Cult.* i. p. 258 *et seq.*, where the authorities are given.)

The Israelites also seem to have possessed ample treasures, for they gave gold freely to Aaron for the golden calf, and gave again as freely, and more than was required, for the Tabernacle. According to the *Talmud* (Kaddishim), the stones of the ephod were of fabulous value. In Solomon's time, also, the gold and silver were as plenteous in Jerusalem as stones. (2 Chronicles 1:15)

4

Inexorable Division

The Holy Tabernacle, a Type or Shadow of the House of God in the Sense of a Community

The next point to which I beg to direct the reader's attention is the extreme severity with which the three Sections of the Tabernacle were separated from each other. The Levites were the appointed servants and ministers of the Court, but from the Holy Place they were excluded on pain of death. The Priests executed the ministry of the Holy Place, but were as solemnly prohibited from venturing beyond the Vail which concealed the Most Holy.

This circumstance deserves earnest consideration. All the three sacerdotal orders were of Levi—Levi, the chosen tribe of a chosen people, the only tribe in Israel to which earthly possessions (*"The Lord spake unto Aaron, Thou shalt have no inheritance in their land, neither shalt thou have any part among them: I am thy part, and thine inheritance among the children of Israel." The Levites had "no inheritance given them among the children of Israel." "Wherefore Levi hath no part, nor inheritance with his brethren; The Lord is his inheritance, according as the Lord thy God promised him." Numbers 18:20, 26:62, Deuteronomy 10:9*) were to be denied during a dispensation in which ample fields, and olive-yards, and vineyards were, if not exclusively, yet as a rule, the rewards of righteousness (*See Note A*); a tribe, too, not permitted to be numbered when the census of the people was commanded to be taken, as if they appertained altogether to a higher sphere (*"And the Lord spoke unto Moses . . . Take ye the sum of all the congregation of the children of Israel after their families, . . . With the number of their names, . . . Only thou shalt not number the tribe of Levi, Neither take the sum of them among the children of Israel. . . For they are wholly given unto Me From among the children of Israel." (Numbers 1:1, 2, 49; 8:16, 8:9-11, 13, 14)*

PRIEST.   HIGH PRIEST.   LEVITE.

And at their mysterious consecration, the whole nation presented them unto God, and laid their hands on their heads exactly as when they offered a common victim in substitution.

"Thou shalt bring the Levites before the Lord:
And the children of Israel shall put their hands upon the Levites;
And Aaron shall offer the Levites for an offering
Of the children of Israel . . .
Thus, shalt thou separate the Levites
From among the children of Israel,
And the Levites shall be Mine." (Numbers 8:10, 11, 14)

They were, in fact, another Israel, for they were expressly chosen instead of all the first born of the people (*See Note B*); and inasmuch as each firstborn was the noble and representative of his house, the Levites were the nobles and divinely elected representatives of this divinely elected people.

Solemn Injunctions

And yet, after all this solemn distinction, they were told that if a Levite laid his hand on any of the sacred vessels of the Holy or Most Holy Places, while such vessel was uncovered, or if he looked on it while in this condition, he had forfeited his life! (*See Note C*)

And if the High Priest put not on his Pallium, or blue robe of the Ephod, with its golden bells (*"And thou shalt make the robe of the ephod all of blue . . . And beneath upon the hem of it thou shalt make pomegranates of blue, of purple, and crimson, and bells of gold between them round about. And it shall be upon Aaron, to minister: and his sound shall be heard when he goth in unto the Holy Place before the Lord, and when he cometh out, that he die not." Exodus 28:31-35*), and thus neglected to warn the ordinary priests performing their services in the Holy Place of his intention to pass through the Vail into the Most Holy, so that they might inadvertently have caught a sight of its mysteries, he, the High Priest, by whose neglect it happened, incurred the penalty of death! (*See Note D*)

Dr. Hook, in his Dictionary, remarks on this subject: "The High Priest probably gave notice to the people (by the sound of his bells) and also desired permission to enter the Sanctuary, and by so doing escaped the punishment of death annexed to an indecent intrusion."

But to me it appears beyond a doubt that the notice which he gave by the sound of his golden bells regarded exclusively the Priests present in the Holy Place; for it is not likely that they could be heard through the Vail of the Holy Place, across the Court of the Priests as far as the Court of Israel; and the object for which they were commanded to be worn, stated in these words,

> "His sound shall be heard
> When he goth into the Holy Place before the Lord,
> And when he cometh out" (Exodus 27:35),

ought to be read in connexon with Leviticus 16:17, where his solemn entrance into *the Holy Place before the Lord is* particularly treated, and where it was commanded,

> "And there shall be no man
> In the Tabernacle of the Congregation:"

viz., the Holy Place, for in the Court many were present during this holy act, and in the Holy Place none could be present but the Priests:

> "When he goth in to make an atonement in the Holy place,
> Until he came out." (Leviticus 16:17)

Clearly, then, the Priests had to be warned off from the Holy Place when the High Priest entered the Most Holy, and this warning was given by the golden bells. And in the absence of distinct Scriptural statements respecting the dread with which the ordinary priest must have shrunk back from the Most Holy, it may be safely argued from the trepidation and forebodings with which the High Priest prepared himself annually for his peculiar functions. (*It may be asked, how were the priests to cover the Ark for removal by the Levites, when the Tabernacle was taken down? The reply is given in Numbers 4:5, 16, and 15, where it is said that Aaron and his sons took down the Vail of the Most Holy, and threw it forward so as to cover the Ark and Cherubim; they then placed two other coverings over it, and allowed the Levites to approach and bear it away. And when the Most Holy of the Temple needed repair, priests who were skilled as craftsmen were let down into it through the ceiling in chests sufficiently open in front to allow them to perform their work, and protecting them at the same time from the light and splendor of the Shekinah." Middoth. c. iv. sect. 5; Leo Jud. De Temple, lib. ii. c. 25, § 236*)

The Divine law respecting those functions and the rules for their performance were stringent and ominous. The High Priest was commanded to come into the Court with a sin-offering, and a burnt- offering to atone for himself and his house—to lay aside his garments of beauty and glory—to bathe his flesh in water, put on white robes, and before venturing to bring the blood of his sacrifice into the Most Holy, to take a censer full of burning coals of fire from the Golden Altar, and his hand full of holy incense beaten small, to bring it within the Vail, and there to put the incense on the burning censer before the Lord, "that the cloud of the incense may cover the Mercy Seat that is upon the testimony, that be die not."

He then retired slowly backward, and after that brought in the sacrificial blood for himself, and again the blood for the atonement of the people. (*The expression in Hebrews 9:7, "into the Second (Holy) went the high priest alone once every year," must be understood of the day—or one day in the year. Philo says that the high priest went twice on the Day of Atonement into the Most Holy, and that if he had entered three times, he would have lost his life; but the Rabbins maintain that he entered four times, but that if he had ventured a fifth time he must have died. Philo, de Legat. ad Caijum, p. 1035; Ioma, ch. v.sect. 1-5; Maimon. de Ingressu in Sanct. c. i. 3*).

It is most instructive to observe how this dread of the Most Holy deepened with the experience of the ancients. The Mishna relates:

> "Seven days before the Day of Atonement the High Priest was removed from his own house to a chamber in the Temple, where he remained for reading, meditation, and prayer. He studied carefully and anxiously the complicated ritual of that solemn day, and on its eve the elders of the great council came to him, and adjured him by Him who dwelt in that Temple not to alter the prescribed services. They took leave of him, and wept, and he took leave of them and wept also."

More and more frequent, it seems, became his ablutions as the term of the dispensation approached. One only was enjoined in the Scripture, but the Mishna speaks of fifteen. Five times he bathed in the Court behind a suspended curtain, ten times he washed hands and feet lest any defilement cleaving to him should put his life in jeopardy when in the Most Holy Place.

If he reached the evening of the Day of Expiation in safety, the nobles conducted him, amidst loud congratulations, to his house; and, in order to manifest his thankfulness to God for having allowed him to pass out of the Most Holy Place in peace, he gave a banquet to his friends. (*Iom.* c. vii. 4.)

Very touching is the allusion to the remarkable circumstance of the High Priest's dread and forebodings on the Day of Atonement, which is contained in the liturgical prayer of the Jews. I extract some of the prayers:

"Behold, how glorious the High Priest was as he came forth from the Most Holy Place unharmed and in peace!"

Very similar is the language of the Book of Ecclesiasticus 1:6, in speaking of the high priest, Simon, the son of Onias, at the same great festival, it should seem:

"How was he honored in the midst of the people in his coming out of the sanctuary!

Like the Tabernacle of the Lord overshadowing the inhabitants of heaven, was the appearance of the High Priest!

He was as the morning star in the midst of a cloud, and as the moon at the full:

As the sun shining upon the temple of the Highest, and as the rainbow giving light in the bright clouds:

And as the flower of roses in the spring of the year, as lilies by the rivers of waters, and as the branches of the frankincense tree in the time of summer:

As fire and incense in the censer, and as a vessel of beaten gold set with all manner of precious stones:

And as a fair olive tree, budding forth fruit, and as a cypress tree which groweth up to the clouds!

When he put on the robe of honor, and was clothed with the perfection of glory, when he went up to the holy altar, he made the garment of holiness honorable!

When he took the portions out of the priest's hands, he himself stood by the grate of the altar compassed with his brethren round about as a young cedar in Libanus, and as palm trees compassed they him round about!

And finishing the service at the altar, . . . he stretched out his hand to the cup, and poured out of the blood of the grape at the foot of the altar. . . Then shouted the sons of Aaron, and sounded the silver trumpets. . . Then all the people together hasted, and fell down to the earth upon their faces, to worship their Lord God Almighty, the Highest."

The Jewish Liturgy for the Day of Atonement says on this last point:

"And when they heard in the Court, how the High Priest pronounced the great and fearful Name, they bowed down and fell on their faces and worshipped before the King of Kings, the Holy One, blessed be His Name!"

"Like lightning glancing from the splendors of God's throne, was the appearance of the High Priest! Like the rainbow in the cloud, was the appearance of the High Priest! As when the sun shineth in his strength, was the appearance of the High Priest! As the dazzling lily in the garden, was the appearance of the High Priest! Like Orion and Seven Planets gleaming in the south, was the appearance of the High Priest! All this was seen whilst the Temple had a standing, and the Most Holy place was firmly founded, and the High Priest did execute his holy services. Blessed be the eye that saw all these things! Verily, the mere mention of them deeply bows down our souls! Blessed be the eye that saw the Holy Tabernacle filled with joyful worshippers! Verily, the mere mention of these things deeply bows down our souls!

Blessed be the eye that saw the scarlet line on the head of the scapegoat turn white as snow! Verily, the memory of these things deeply bows down our souls! And now, O God, it is well known before Thee, and the throne of Thy glory, it is not with us as in days past—we have no High Priest."

A Time of Great Peril

In their prayers therefore the fact is treated as well known, that great peril threatened the High Priest on the Day of Atonement. Of exactly the same import also is a passage in the Mishna, which treats, *es professo*, of the Day of Expiation, as celebrated in the ancient Temple.

> "The outer Vail of the Most Holy was slightly withdrawn on the south side, and the inner Vail of the Most Holy was raised on the north side. He, the High Priest, stepped between the two northward, turned southward . . . set down the censer close to the staves of the Ark, and waited until the whole Temple was filled with the smoke of the incense. He then retired as he had entered, and offered a short prayer in the Holy Place. He did not remain long to pray lest his long absence should terrify the people." (*Iom.* c. v. § 2.)

Nor are there traditions wanting to show that some High Priest perished in the Temple on the Day of Atonement. (See Sheringh. in *Iom.* 0. vii. §§ 2, 3, 4.) In the absence of direct passages of Holy Scripture to show that the common priest was excluded from the Most Holy as peremptorily as the Levites were excluded from the Holy Place, do not the solemn preparation of the High Priest, and the dread and trepidation with which he drew near that inner Temple, prove the stern exclusion of the inferior order? For if, under the shield of God's express command, the High Priest approached the Most Holy with faltering and fearful step, how could the ordinary priest, who had no such law to plead for his temerity, hope to penetrate unharmed the mysteries of the second Vail?

This, then, is the proposition that I would derive from these statements, and impress distinctly on the reader, that the three sections of the Tabernacle, though divided only by thin Vails, were sharply separated from each other, and none of the ministers of the lower division were permitted to pass into the higher.

Three Stages of the Church

And if again we look from the type to the antitype, we shall perceive what gave rise to this inexorable separation. I have already referred to the reason for the three divisions of the Tabernacle. At the period of its erection in the wilderness, three distinct epochs, dispensations, or stages of development, were before the Church— namely, that of the Law, of the Gospel, and of Glory. Only into the first of these she had then entered, but the other two loomed in the future, and hence the need in the Church's type or shadow to exhibit this ternary division.

And scarcely less simple and obvious is the reason for the sharp separation of these divisions.

The Law—with its gorgeous pageantry of worship, its grand temple, its music, its priests in their grand robes, their grand festivals, and still grander ritual—the Law, with its solemn prophets, and their striking and impressive parabolical acting; prophets, often invested with terrible and miraculous power—with its swift demonstrations of God's anger and approval—was the Church's schoolmaster to lead her to Christ. Without it, she could not have learned the rudiments of faith, or been prepared for the higher dispensation.

This Christian dispensation, on the other hand—so undemonstrative, and with its perplexing silence of God—with its glorious fulness of the Holy Ghost, who comes, however, without observation, on whose silent pinions, too, Christ enters the heart as silently and as meekly as when He entered Jerusalem as King—working within us in all stillness the understanding of His silent or humbly spoken word—without more prophecy, without gorgeous pageantry of worship, without startling, striking miracles, without swift demonstrations of Divine displeasure or approval; this silent economy is, as you may argue from its very existence, the indispensable preparation for the next, where souls shall take rank in the eternal hierarchy of glory as they have been faithful to their now silent and unseen God.

Thus, impressive demonstration, suited to the Church's minority, was the precursor of God's higher, but silent work suited to the dignity of the Church's manhood, and His silent work, recognized and received in faith, is the forerunner of wondrous demonstration in endless glory.

But it may be objected, Did not the saints of the Old Testament anticipate much of our standing by faith? and may not we, in like manner, enter even now into the enjoyment of the glorious future?

In like manner, yes! by faith, but not in actual fruition!

Instances are, indeed, not wanting to prove that the subjects of a lower dispensation may desire, and even attempt to grasp, the distinctive prerogatives of a future and higher dispensation; but God either fearfully rebuked this temerity, as in the mournful instance of Korah (*See Note E*), and the princes of his faction; or else He vouchsafed not the premature petition, as when

> "Many prophets and kings
> Desired to see those things which we see,
> And did not see them;
> And to hear those things which we hear,
> And did not hear them." (Luke 10:24)

Attempts not very unlike these have been adventured from the earliest ages of Christianity up to the present time, and for men's willful and wicked blindness as to the real nature of this economy, will in all likelihood continue to be adventured to the end of time. Men have manifested in countless ways their impatience of Christ's easy yoke, and fretting at the humiliations that beset the Christian's path have affected pardon and the assurance of Heaven without real holiness of life; have forestalled in this Dispensation of humiliation the exalted prerogatives of the Church in the fulness of glory—her future spotless perfection in the individual and community; her lofty and perfect wisdom when she shall know as she is known; and her limitless power and universal sway when all things shall be put under her; and God only knows whether these and other like attempts take rank with Korah's proud rebellion, or the proleptic aspirations of those faithful kings and prophets and righteous men; but this is absolutely certain—the attempts have been made, and have been disappointed.

The dispensations are separated from each other in a manner which is admirably foreshadowed by those significant textures, the linen Vails which divided the Court from the Holy Place, and that from the Most Holy.

The Vail of the Holy Place was rent in twain when the death of Christ terminated the dispensation of shadows and opened the kingdom of Heaven to all believers. The dispensation itself had faded away

"Like a wreath of mist at eve,"

and the Church found herself standing in her present higher economy before even her holiest members were aware of the transition. It required years and many special revelations to convince even the apostles that the dispensation of the Law had passed away. But the second Vail, which separates us from the Most Holy, is there still, and preaches our exclusion. Faith has lifted it sometimes and caught glimpses of its unutterable splendor; and Hope casts her anchor there, as it is written:

> "Which hope we have
> As an anchor of the soul,
> Both sure and steadfast,
> And which entereth into that within the Vail;
> Whither the forerunner is for us entered,
> Even Jesus,
> Made an High Priest for ever after the order of Melchisedec."
> (Hebrews 11:19-20)

The Savior is there visibly present, surrounded by our holy dead,

> "By the general assembly of the Church of the First-born,
> Which are written in Heaven...
> The spirits of just men made perfect...
> And an innumerable company of angels." (Hebrews 12:23)

(Alford says on this passage: "Mount Sion, the abode of God, which He loved, and where He will abide continually, is [here] used to signify, not its mere representation which men know by that name, but the reality, God's own abode in Heaven... He is its Maker and Builder... and evermore dwells in it with the light of His presence... And in it are the spirits of just men made perfect—the whole number of the just who have passed into their rest, from righteous Abel downwards.")

But we, the living, must abide without until death raises that Vail, or the advent of the Lord takes it away. However, its final removal is imminent.

Whilst these lines are being read, God's saints now living on this earth may be summoned—perhaps, at the first notes of the last trumpet—perhaps, shortly before it—to enter into the Holiest of all, to be suddenly invested with all the attributes of glory in the presence of the Lord and the blest departed.

But He only that commanded the suspension of the Vails can remove them, and until so removed, these frail partitions exclude each lower state from the higher as though they were walls of adamant, and on their front seems written—

"Learn to labor, and to wait."

These, then, being the facts of the case, it was manifestly right that the Tabernacle, the type and shadow of the Church, should be marked by three divisions, and that these divisions should have been separated, as they were, with inexorable rigidity.

NOTE A

"Blessed be the man that feared the Lord,
That delighted greatly in His commandments...
Wealth and riches shall be in his house..." (Psalm 112:1-3)

"God give thee of the dew of heaven upon thy fields,
The fatness of the earth,
And plenty of corn and wine." (Genesis 27:28)

"And O, Naphtali, satisfied with favor,
And full with the blessing of the Lord:
Possess thou the west and the south." (Deuteronomy 33:23)

"And it shall come to pass,
If thou hearken diligently unto the voice of the Lord thy God . . .
To observe and to do all His commandments
Which I command thee this day,
That the Lord thy God will set thee on high
Above all the nations of the earth:

And all these blessings shall come on thee, and overtake thee,
If thou shalt hearken unto the voice of the Lord thy God... (Deuteronomy 28:1-2)

"The Lord shall make thee plenteous in goods...
And in the fruit of thy ground,
In the land which the Lord swear unto thy fathers to give thee."
(Deuteronomy 28:11)

NOTE B

"For they are wholly given unto Me from
Among the children of Israel;
Instead of such as open every Womb,
Even instead of the 'first-born
Of all the children of Israel have I taken them unto Me.
For all the first-born of Israel are Mine....
On the day that I smote every first-born in the land of Egypt
I sanctified them for Myself.
And I have taken the Levites
For all the first-born of the children of Israel." (Numbers 8:16-18)

NOTE C

"And when Aaron and his sons
Have made an end of covering the Sanctuary,
And all the vessels of the Sanctuary,
As the camp is to set forward;
After that the sons of Kohath shall come to bear it;
But they shall not touch any holy thing, lest they die....
And the Lord spoke unto Moses and unto Aaron, saying,
Cut yet not off the tribe of the families
Of the Kohathites from among the Levites:

But thus, do unto them, that they may *live*, and *not die*,
When they approach unto the most holy things:
Aaron and his sons shall go in and appoint them
Every one to his service, and to his burden:
But they shall not go in to see when the holy things are covered,
Lest they die." (Numbers 4:15, 17-20)

NOTE D

The number of these bells the Scriptures do not mention, but the Jewish Fathers estimate them at seventy-two (Maimon. *De Vas Sanct.* c. 9); Clement of Alexandria, at three hundred and sixty-five (Strom. v. p. 56%); and some others at fifty, or twelve, &c. (Polydor. Virgil. *de Invent. Rer.* l. iv. 5). But only of real importance seems the question when the High Priest wore the robe with its golden bells.

Careless writers on this subject have asserted that he went with them into the Most Holy Place on every day of Atonement; but this is not true. Into the Most Holy he entered only, robed in white, without the robe of the ephod, and therefore without the bells. To what purpose, then, was the robe with bells, and their warning sound? The traditions of Rabbins on this subject are too absurd to be mentioned. And if he ministered merely in the Court and Holy Place with his golden robes and bells, what need was there in warning off the Levites or the priests from their respective spheres of duty?

Certainly, the command respecting the bells contained in Exodus was given before Aaron was precluded from entering often into the Most Holy. And when, as Leviticus 16:1 implies, he entered the Most Holy as often as his inclination led him, it is intelligible that he should have been commanded to warn the priests, who were frequently in the Holy Place, of his approach to the inner mysteries.

But then the bells formed a permanent integral part of the High Priest's vestments, "for glory and beauty," and the command for their use was of perpetual obligation; yet if his entrance with them into the Most Holy ceased with the death of Nadab and Abihu (Leviticus 16:1), they were ever after useless, and the command respecting them unmeaning. This cannot be. That the High Priest entered, on pressing national affairs, into the Most Holy, to ask counsel of God by the Urim and Thummim, has been asserted, but is most uncertain. The right solution of the question is manifestly as follows: On the day of Atonement the High Priest first put on his golden robes with the robe of the ephod and its bells. In these he performed the morning sacrifice. He then washed, and put on his white robes. Tradition speaks of repeated changes of these vestments. It says that in the morning of the day of Atonement the High Priest's white robes were of costliest Pelusian linen.

In these he offered his own sacrifice, entered with incense into the Most Holy, and afterwards with blood.

In these also he read to the people the passage of Holy Scripture beginning with the words:

> "And the Lord spoke unto Moses, after the death of the two sons of Aaron" (Leviticus 16:1); or, if he preferred it, he read in a white surplice of his own. He again put off his white robes, washed, put on his golden robes, and offered the goat for the sin-offering. . . He washed again, put on his white robes—this time of finest Indian linen —entered once more into the Most Holy, . . . washed again, and put on his golden robes, in which he completed the services of the day. (See Jarchi, in Leviticus 16:23, and Jom. cc. ii., iii., v.)

But however, these changes of vestments and these washings were multiplied as time wore on, it appears that, according to Holy Scripture, the usage as regards his change of vestments was originally much simpler.

The High Priest entered with his golden garments into the Holy Place, and the sound of the bells apprised the priests of his entrance.

There he put off his golden garments, washed in a golden bason (*Iom.* c. iv., sect. 5), put on his white robes, and entered into the Most Holy. Thence he returned, assumed his golden robes, and went out to the people into the Court.

Such seems the plain sense of the words:

> "There shall be no man in the Tabernacle of the congregation,
> When he goth in to make an atonement in the Holy Place,
> Until he goeth out...
> And Aaron shall come into the Tabernacle of the congregation,
> And shall put off the linen garments
> Which he put on when he went into the Holy Place,
> And shall leave them there;
> And he shall wash his flesh in water in the Holy Place,
> And put on his (golden) garments, and come forth."
> (Leviticus 16:17, 23-24)

The bells thus warned the priests of the High Priest's impending entrance into the Most Holy; nor were they permitted to re-enter until the bells announced to them that the solemn office was at an end.

At the Vail outside, the captain of the Temple and the priests on duty seem also to have waited on ordinary days when the High Priest chose to minister, nor did they raise the Vail until his approaching footsteps apprised them of the termination of his service. (See *Tamid*, c. vii. sect. 1.)

NOTE E

Korah was of the tribe of Levi, the sacerdotal tribe which represented the nation in the service of God, instead of the first-born.

The consecration of the first-born to God's service, and the offering of the firstlings of the flock and herd, and of first-fruits, appears to have been the subject of primeval revelation, for they were practiced before any recorded injunction on the subject. Thus, Cain brought of the first-fruits of the ground an offering unto the Lord; Abel brought of the firstlings of his flock; and Esau is rebuked for despising his birthright. (Genesis 4:3-4; 25:34)

But this consecration of the first-born of man, and the offering of firstlings and first-fruits, was afterwards expressly commanded in Israel— e.g., Exodus 13:11-12:

> "And it shall come to pass,
> When the Lord shall bring thee
> Into the land of the Canaanites ...
> That thou shalt set apart unto the Lord
> All that opened the matrix,
> And every firstling that cometh of a beast which thou hast."

All the firstlings of pure animals were sacrificed to God; and after the election of the tribe of Levi, all the first-born of man was redeemed with money.

> "I sacrifice to the Lord all that opened the matrix, being males;
> But all the first-born of my children I redeem." (Exodus 13:15)

The fruits of the fields were devoted in like manner.

"Thou shalt not delay to offer the first of thy ripe fruits
And of thy liquors:
The first-born of thy sons shalt thou give to Me." (Exodus 22:29)

By this consecration the Church and all her earthly possessions were uplifted into a sphere of sanctity, as specially belonging to God, and were protected and enriched by His peculiar blessing. Of this sanctity of men and things, Paul speaks when he says:

"If the first-fruit be holy, the lump also is holy." (Romans 11:16)

And that a special blessing rested on all thus consecrated by the offering the first-born, may perhaps be argued from the circumstance that evil sent on the first-born was the certain presage of misfortune to the family to which he belonged; a law terribly illustrated by the fact that shortly after the first-born of the Egyptians had been miraculously destroyed, the king and the flower of that nation sank as lead into the mighty waters.

But besides the fact, that in the first-born the family to which he belonged became God's own, and rested in the shadow of His special protection, the first-born also represented his family as its priest. According to the ancient Jewish tradition, the first-born is spoken of when God commanded Moses, before the call of Aaron, to the priesthood. "And let the priests also which come near the Lord sanctify themselves." (Exodus 19:22) And then Moses, in Exodus 24:3, "sent young men to offer burnt-offerings and peace-offerings of oxen before the Lord." See the Jewish authorities in Selden, lib. (Ze saw. in bona defunct. c. 5; so also, in Alford, in Heb. xii. 22, 24): "The first-born in Israel were dedicated to God, especially as His priests" In their first-born the people of Israel saw their high national vocation reflected.

But, for reasons not stated, God chose to diminish the religious privileges of the first-born, and to transfer them thus diminished to the tribe of Levi. The conjectures for this transfer offered by Jewish and Christian writers are manifold, but have no positive foundation in Holy Scripture. But the transfer itself was clearly and repeatedly commanded: *e. g.,*

> "And behold,
> I have taken the Levites from among the children of Israel,
> Instead of all the first-born . . . . ." (Numbers 3:12, 40, 41, 45)

Their representatives had lost the functions of the priesthood proper, which the first-born had possessed, and became merely the servants of the priests. The first-born of Israel was paired off with the Levites; not with the family in which the proper functions of the priesthood were executed; and when the number of the first-born in Israel exceeded by two hundred threescore and thirteen the number of Levites, those of the priestly family were not permitted to complete the deficiency. (Numbers 3:46) In the Levites "given as a gift to Aaron and to his sons . . . to do the service, (or the servant's work) in the Tabernacle, the people (Numbers 8:19) read their divine standing.

The priesthood once really theirs, was now, for high economic reasons, taken from them, but held out to them again in promise, to be fulfilled in the undefined future. It is very important to observe this. Shortly before the loss of the priesthood by the first-born to Aaron they were told (Exodus 19:5-6):

> "If ye will obey my voice indeed,
> And keep my covenant,
> Then ye shall be a peculiar treasure unto me above all people:
> For all the earth is mine:
> And ye shall be unto me a kingdom of priests."

In the Aaronic priesthood they saw their future standing. And it was in sad but terrible consistency with this conditional promise, that, when after the schooling of ages, they had not complied with the indispensable condition affixed to the promise, the language of prophecy revokes, for a period at least, the prospective advancement; and Hosea is commissioned to tell them:

> "Because thou hast rejected knowledge,
> I will also reject thee,
> That thou shalt be no priest to me." (Hosea 4:6)

Yet when the time had fully come for a national priesthood, the faithful remnant of Israel received the sacerdotal appellation; and Peter, the apostle of the circumcision, writing to the Diaspora, or the Israel scattered abroad through the world says—

> "Ye . . . as lively stones,
> Are built up a. spiritual house,
> An holy priesthood." (1 Peter 2:5)

But the rebellion of Korah consisted in their proudly refusing the position of Levites and aspiring to that of the Aaronic priesthood, before the nation whom the Levites were chosen to represent was prepared for the advancement. And this fretting impatience preventing their preparing themselves effectually for the position they affected—and if the impatience spread to the nation, preventing the possibility of its ever attaining its higher destiny—led to Korah's dreadful punishment. The Levites were essentially servants, and reflected in this estate the condition of the Church under the Law, for

> "The heir, as long as he is a child,
> Differeth nothing from a servant." (Galatians 4:1)

And the Levites were poor; they had no territorial possessions, and are always classed with the stranger, the fatherless, and the widow. Passages like the following occur repeatedly:

> "Thou shalt not forsake the Levite:
> For he hath no part nor inheritance with thee.
> At the end of three years thou shalt bring forth all the tithe
> Of thine increase of the same year,
> And shalt lay it up within thy gates:
> And the Levite, because he hath no part
> Nor inheritance with thee,
> And the stranger, and the fatherless,
> And the widow, which are within thy gates,
> Shall come, and shall eat and be satisfied;
> That the Lord thy God may bless thee in all the
> Work of thine hand which thou doest."
> (Deuteronomy 14:27-29)

And their poverty reminded the nation, even in that dispensation of worldly promises, that it was a nobler attainment to become poor for the service of God than to seek earthly riches; and their office as teachers—for the Levites were divinely-appointed religious teachers—hinted to the devout in Israel that they must go and proclaim their God to the ends of the earth.

And how effectually many of them learned this is best argued from the fact, that wherever they were carried in their voluntary or compulsory wanderings, the light of God sprang up in the darkness of paganism: thus, *e. g.*, their influence is clearly traceable in the Zenda—Vesta, in the earliest hymns of the Hindoo, and in classic poetry;—and who shall say how much these Wanderers had to do in preparing the nations among whom they lived for the heralds of the Cross?

Nor is it unworthy of notice, that our Lord came at the close of the Jewish Dispensation in the Levitical character.

He, like the Levite, was a servant, for it is written,

> "He made Himself of no reputation,
> And took upon Him the form of a servant." (Philippians 2:7)

And, like the Levite, He for our sakes became poor—so poor, that He exclaimed,

> "Foxes have holes,
> And the birds of the air have nests,
> But the Son of man hath not where to lay His head." (Luke 9:58)

And to complete the analogy, He came as a Teacher. The Levites were not allowed to sprinkle the blood of sacrifices—that was one of the priest's characteristic functions; and when the Lord shed His own most precious Blood, He had entered upon His Priesthood.

But as the Levite only saw the sprinkling of the atoning blood of their legal sacrifices, even so did the Church of the Mosaic economy witness at its close the effusion of that Blood to which all legal sacrifices pointed.

JERUSALEM THE GOLDEN

THE COURT

5

Symbolical Forms

The Tabernacle, a Type of the Church's Local Habitation

I approach now a more difficult, but neither less beautiful nor less suggestive symbolism; viz., the figurative meaning of the numbers which mark the structure of the Tabernacle.

My chief difficulty lies in the distrust with which this special symbolism is regarded, arising partly from the abstruse appearance of the subject, and partly, principally perhaps, from the seemingly absurd and often most arbitrary and fanciful manner in which it has been treated.

I shall endeavor to keep this in mind, and to state what has to be said in order to explain my point, with all possible clearness: and my task is simplified by the fact that all the mystic numbers connected with the Tabernacle and its ritual, whether embodied in forms or not, resolve themselves into the two factors of the confessedly symbolical seven—the numbers three and four; and, strictly speaking, I have to deal only with one of these.

For the sake of clearness, however, I shall glance at both; and my first endeavor must be to show how very prominently they are brought before us in connection with my subject.

The Usage of Threes

Three metals, brass, silver, and gold, were commanded to mark and distinguish the three divisions of the structure; three doorways which led to them were hung with three Vails embroidered with three mystic colors. Three holy things were placed in the Most Holy—the Ark, the Mercy-seat, and Cherubim; three in the Holy Place—the Altar of Incense, the Golden Candlestick, and Table; and three, as some regard it, in the Court—the Altar, the Laver, and " *his Foot*'." (Exodus 30:18, 38:8, 39:39) (*The three divisions symbolized certainly the three economies of the Spiritual Prototype; but then, why and whence that original ternary division? Tertullian says: "All things in nature are prophetic lineaments of Divine operations, God not merely speaking parables, but doing them." Quoted by Trench, On the Parables, p. 12. This thought is well put in Johnson's Explanation of Scripture Prophecies (1742), p. 228: "God, before the world was made, foreseeing the fall, and designing the redemption of man, may reasonably be supposed, at the time of creation, or in the contrivance and formation of things, to have had a special eye and regard to that future renovation: so that these things which appear to us to come to pass only according to the invariable laws or stated course of nature might be predetermined by an all-wise God ... as monetory signs, emblems, and figures of some ... transactions in the moral world. And if the works of nature may be subservient to such designs, or made to carry some mystical meaning in them, much more may the works of His Providence, which are free and unrestrained."*)

Three sacred orders were ordained to perform the service of the Tabernacle; three mystic colors marked the girdle of each priest; three times a year holy festivals were kept, when every man in Israel must present himself before God; and the festivals themselves pointed respectively to God the Son (Passover), to God the Holy Ghost (Pentecost), and to God the Father (Tabernacles, or the Feast of Ingathering at the end of all things), when the Son Himself shall be subject to the Father, and God be all in all. (*"Then cometh the end, When He shall have delivered up the kingdom to God, Even the Father; When He shall have put down all rule and all authority and power. For He must reign till He hath put all enemies under His feet . . . And when all things shall be subdued unto Him, Then shall the Son also Himself be subject unto Him That put all things under Him, That God may be all in all." (1 Corinthians 15:24-25, 28)*

In three groups of three each were the mystic ornaments set in the twice three branches of the golden Candlestick, and in four groups of three in its shaft; three rows of precious stones, four in each row, shone in the breastplate of the High Priest; and three times four consecrated loaves of shewbread lay on the golden Table. Three great divisions formed the ancient church—the Tent of God, or Sanctuary, the Tents of the Levites, and the Tents of Israel; and three tribes were joined in each of the four encampments in which the holy people were marshalled round their mystic temple, stretching out, as ancient tradition says, three times four miles towards each of the four points of heaven, to foreshadow the Church universal which should be gathered from the four corners of the earth.

The Meaning of Fours

Four pillars, standing in four brazen sockets, formed the entrance of the Court; four pillars, set in sockets of silver, the entrance to the Most Holy; four curtains hung over the Sanctuary, the lowermost of which consisted of ten smaller ones, each of which measured four cubits in breadth, and four times seven (3+4) cubits in length; four horns surmounted the golden Altar, and the altar of burnt-offerings—four gums, or tears, as the Greeks called them, composed the holy incense; four ingredients the oil for consecration; branches of four kinds of trees were waved in the Temple, and are still waved in their synagogues at the Feast of Tabernacles; and of the same four trees were their bowers or booths constructed at that festival, to symbolize the restored and thence-forward imperishable glories of Paradise. (*Pythagoras, so says*

Suidas, taught that ten is the compound of four, because it is contained in four; viz., one + two + three + itself = 10. The Decas, or ten, is therefore the developed or perfect four, and both four and ten were ancient numerical symbols of the world. Plut. de Is. et Os., c. 76. Protopathic. in Hesiodic dies, &c),

Four were the sacred vestments of the common priest, twice four those of the High Priest; four-square, i. e. presenting the four in form or geometrical embodiment, were the four times twelve pillars of the four-square Sanctuary: four-square the three Vails, four-square the four curtains, the Breastplate, the Altars, the Golden Table, the Ark, and the Mercy Seat, which was overshadowed by four wings; four-square also were the Court, the Holy Place, and the Most Holy.

What can it mean that our Holy God revealed these numbers with such precision and care, and commanded their strict embodiment in the erection of this symbolical structure and the establishment of its Ritual?

Canon Wordsworth says, in reference to the mystic numbers of the Apocalypse:

> "Let us not imagine that these numbers are superfluous and without meaning. Nothing in Scripture is. We cannot now understand all the harmonies of the Divine arithmetic. Yet some we can."

Shall less be claimed for the Numbers of the Tabernacle? Why should it?

The Cabalists, whose profound acquaintance with the Hebrew Scriptures no one will call in question, asserted this Divine arithmetic in reference to every portion of the Old Testament.

"Woe be to him," said a contemporary of the apostle John, "who imagines that the Holy Word of God contains nothing but the letter. . . If angels when sent down to earth are forced to clothe themselves with a body . . . for the purpose of enabling man to perceive them, how much more necessary was it that the Word of God, which created the angels, and all worlds besides, should assume a body when revealing Himself to mankind? The letter of the Scriptures is this body, and if any man shall say there is nothing deeper in it, let him have no part in the life to come." (*Soh*. fol. 152a.)

For all Holy Scripture they claimed a threefold meaning, viz., the literal, spiritual, and secret or mystic; and one mode by which they read the last was numerical symbolism.

The Fathers also adopted this mode of interpretation, but with less knowledge of Hebrew, and with much less depth. Some examples from the latter, in their exposition of the New Testament, and a few passages to show how modern divines have handled this grand subject, the reader will find at the end of this chapter (*See Note A*).

But there must be some plain, practical common-sense way of stating this abstruse matter; for all other things, when rightly understood, are capable of being thus stated. The way in this case seems to be this. The emblematical use of numbers and of their embodiment in geometrical or conventional forms reaches back far into pagan antiquity, and seems to have originated as follows:

The knowledge of the true God, according 'to the testimony of Holy Scripture, was originally universal. The histories of Abraham, of Job, and Balaam, imply this knowledge; and so does the language of the apostle Paul, when he says of the whole heathen world, that:

> "They knew God,
> But glorified Him not as God,
> Neither were thankful;
> But became vain in their imaginations,

And their foolish heart was darkened....
And as they did not like to retain God in their knowledge,
God gave them over to a reprobate mind." (Romans 1:21, 28)

(*"God came to Abimelech in a dream by night, And said to him, Behold, thou art but a dead man, For the woman which thou hast taken; For she is a man's wife. But Abimelech .... said, Lord, wilt thou slay also a righteous nation? Said he not unto me, She is my sister? And she, even she herself said, He is my brother: In the integrity of my heart And innocence of my hands have I done this. And God said unto him ... Yea, I knew that thou didst this in the integrity of thy heart." Genesis 20:3, 6. Here then some two thousand years before Christ, we meet with the knowledge of the true God in Egypt—communion with Him spoken of as a matter of ordinary occurrence, and uprightness in king and nation even before God. Their decline was indeed fearfully rapid; but how immeasurably higher was the Egypt of Abimelech than that of Isis and Osiris, whose incestuous relationships prevented not their deification; and how far superior also to the most refined period of the most gifted people of the later pagan world, in whose midst Plato taught the community of wives. "Melchizedek, king of Salem .... Was the Priest of the Most High God." Genesis 14:18. Job, probably a contemporary of Abraham, exclaims, "I have heard of thee By the hearing of the ear; But now mine eye seeth thee, Wherefore I abhor myself, And repent in dust and ashes."... "I know that my Redeemer liveth." Job 42:5-6, 19:25. Balaam says: "If Balak would give me his house full of silver and gold; I cannot go beyond the word of the Lord My God to do less or more," and it is said of him:"He knew the knowledge of the Highest, And saw the vision of the Almighty." Numbers 22:18; 24:26. Clearly then, the Scriptures teach us that, in the early ages of mankind the knowledge of the true God was universal, and the traces of this knowledge meet us everywhere in pagan antiquity*).

HERMAN DOUGLAS

Numbers in Pagan Religions

The world once knew God—God the absolute and personal One—God the Triunal: but as in the sad history of Unitarianism we have seen the terminology and symbols of Christianity retained by men among whom the distinctive doctrines of our faith had been lost; and holy names transferred to fictions, and the Sacraments celebrated in empty mimicry; so did words and signs that had belonged to man's primeval faith survive the general apostasy, and came to be applied—not always perhaps without a glimpse of their original significance—to Nature and her subservient forces.

And as in Unitarianism, instances have been, when old words and symbols compelled some earnest and deeper minds to return to Christianity; so uttered, those ancient words and symbols...

> "That warning still and deep
> At which high spirits of old would start
> E'en from their pagan sleep..."

And facilitated the restoration of man's ancient creed by the apostles and their followers.

There is but *One*—one First Cause, faltered in blindness the Egyptian hierophant—it is Kneph, the air—intelligent air! Some whispered; and he construed Nature as a Trinity: Isis, the Moon (*Plutarch, De Is. et Os. 4*), or sometimes the Nile; Osiris the Earth, or the Sun; and Typhon the fierce Simoom of the Desert, or the Sea, or anything fatal to Isis or Osiris.

On the Temple of Isis, at Sais, was the inscription—strange memory of lost Truth!—"I am all that is, and was, and is to come!"—her image bore a three-leaved flower on its head, the emblem of Divinity; and when worshippers approached her with a four-barred sistrum, to signify the concord and music of creation which she was believed to have formed out of four elements,

> "The eldest birth
> Of Nature's womb, that in quaternion run
> Perpetual circles multiform; and mix
> And nourish all things, not without harmony."

The black Apis, their representative of Osiris, bore a beetle, the emblem of his creative power, on his tongue; and a white square, the symbol of creation, on his forehead. Herod. iii. 28. (*Some read it a triangle— another emblem of Divinity*).

The Magi repeated as unconsciously the primeval traditions, and called the source of all things Zeruana Akarene, which some render eternity; others, on account of Herodotus's testimony, infinite space; and they also spoke of a Trinity—Ormuzd, the good in creation, Ahriman, the evil, and Honover the Word, or Mithra, love, the mediator between the two contending principles. Both the equilateral triangle and the square were their emblems of Mithra, who was represented as speeding through infinity upon a chariot drawn by four steeds—the symbols of the elements (*Payne Knight, on Symbolic Language, sect. 222, p. 182; Laur. Lydus de Mens. (Roth) i. p. 210. Dion. Chrys. quoted by Bahr, i. 166*).

At Tak-Khesra, they found an ancient Babylonian monument, which represented Deity under the emblem of three stars, and from the central star four rays were projected, to signify the procession of all things from God.

The Hindoo called the One Source of all, Parahbrahm, the negation of nothingness, ' fiction not unlike the Hegelian god; and their Trimurti, or Trinity, are—Brahma, the self-unfolding, or the sun; Vishnu, the air; and Sceva, fire, or the destructive principle. The triangle, with its apex pointing upward to heaven, was their hieroglyph of Vishnu; and the triangle pointing down-ward, their hieroglyph of Sceva.

The four-leaved lotus was both an Egyptian and Hindoo emblem of creation, and even the Chinese are said to have a name for God, Tao, signifying One in three; and to have laid out their finest province in the form of a triangle, subdivided into three smaller triangles, in honor of Deity.

But notice how their numerical symbols prepared the pagan world for the return of primeval truth.

There is but *One* First Cause, taught Anaximander, 600 13.0., that One is Air.

There is but One from which all things rise, and to which all return, said Thales, 550 B.C., and that One is Water.

There is One, taught Hesiod. It is the Unfathomable; and his Trinity was the Earth, Hell, and Love. From him, too, may the saying have been derived:

> "The Unfathomable was sealed up in night, until light penetrated and illumined it. This light parted itself in three rays, and these three are One—the unseen God, who made all things." (Creutz. *Symb.* iv. p. 82.)

Pythagoras and Plato travelled into far countries and must have come in contact with Divine revelation. They taught:

- The Monas, or One, is underived, and therefore the sign of the Self-Existent and Absolute!
- The Duas, or two, is the first product of the Monas, and therefore the emblem of matter proceeding from God—matter, they

added as in sorrow, alienated from God, and in opposition to Him—and therefore also the sign of strife and division.
- The Trias, or three, reunites the divided one and two, and is therefore the real One—the symbol of all beauty and perfection. The Trias, and the equilateral triangle, said Pythagoras, is the elementary source of all created things. Three, said Plato, is the signature of Deity, who is the beginning, the Center, and end of all things.

Three, then, and four, and their geometrical and conventional signs, were respectively the universal, ancient emblems of God and the world.

The Scriptural Use of Numbers

And the Holy Scriptures tacitly justify and assume this traditional symbolism as they assume many of the primeval traditions —e. g., the Divine origin of sacrifice (*Genesis 4:3*), the implied vicarious suffering, and the consequent atonement (*Genesis 4:7*); the distinction between clean and unclean animals (*Genesis 7:2*); nay, the very Being of God (*Genesis 1:1*), and His subsistence as a Trinity (*Genesis 1:1 — Elohim*).

Thus, the number three is used in the Old Testament not merely to denote quantity, but divine things, and "godlike" persons.

In Proverbs 22:20, we translate this numeral (*Sheloshim, literally triangular. 1. Fuerst, Conc. Heb. s. v., "quid-quid tres angulos habit."—LXX, threefold*) by *excellent things*, but Fuerst explains it to mean "*mighty, marvelous,* and *mysterious matters.*"

In Ezekiel 23:14-15 we translate the same word by Prince:

> "When she saw men portrayed upon the wall,
> The images of the Chaldeans portrayed with vermilion,

> Girded with girdles upon their loins,
> Exceeding in dyed attire upon their heads,
> All of them princes to look to."

And in verse 23, we render it *great lords:*

> "The Babylonians, and all the Chaldeans, ... all of them,
> Great lords and renowned."

In 2 Kings 2:17-19, we translate it *lord,* and in Exodus 14:7 and 15:4, captains, where the Chaldees has Gaborim, mighty men or princes, and the *Septuagint* tristate or powerful nobles.

To say that these princes were described by the numeral because third in rank, is a baseless conjecture devised to dispose of a difficulty, the solution of which is sufficiently easy when the symbolical usage of the number three, which pervaded all antiquity, is frankly taken into account.

Besides, how can the passage in Proverbs be explained on the assumption of third in order?

We should then have to read it, "Have I not written to thee third-rate things in counsel and knowledge,"—an interpretation which amounts to a reduction ad absurdum.

But on the view I contend for, that this numeral stands for Divine, the passage is clear and forcible.

Nor is it at all against the genius of Holy Scripture, or exceptional, to describe distinguished human beings by divine appellations.

Thus, we read *Ele Moab,* which we translate the mighty men of Moab, in Exodus 15:; but which literally means the gods of Moab.

So also, in Ezekiel 12:12-13:

> "The King of Babylon is come to Jerusalem,
> And hath taken the king thereof....
> He hath also taken the mighty (lit. the gods) of the land."

And so again in Ezekiel 32:21:

> "The strong among the mighty (lit. the gods) shall speak to him."

Here, then, we have a name which in some two hundred instances is distinctly applied to God in Holy Scripture as deliberately applied to great nobles and chieftains.

And in these instances, Ele and *Shelishe* are treated as synonymous in Chaldees, Greek, and English.

And if still other examples are wanted where the Scriptures give Divine names to human beings, let me remind the reader of the well-known passages:

> "And the Lord said unto Moses,
> See, I have made thee a god to Pharaoh." (Exodus 7:1); and
> "I have said ye are gods." (Psalm 82:6)

To me it seems that the usage of the epithet "triple," for Divine, given to single individuals, points back to a period when the knowledge of God as One and Three, or Triune, was familiar to the Church, perhaps to mankind; and this impression is still further confirmed by the fact that both in Holy Scripture and immemorial tradition the number Three is symbolically used in reference to God and His service.

Thus, Aaron and his sons, when blessing the people in God's name day by day, and according to an inspired formula (Numbers 6:22-27) pronounced the ineffable Name three times, and in so doing are said to have raised three fingers to Heaven, as if pointing the people to the Triune God from whom the benediction had now descended.

This custom, the origin of which is lost in dim antiquity, is still most rigorously observed among the Jewish people.

The Seraphim which Isaiah saw in the Immediate Presence, as if to proclaim the Sanctity of each Person of the Holy Trinity, cried in the Prophet's hearing,

> "Holy, Holy, Holy,
> The Lord of Hosts!" (Isaiah 6:3)

(*"Is," which the English version adds before the Lord, is an interpolation which weakens the force of the original*).

The living Creatures or Cherubim which the apostle John sees in and round the Throne of God re-echo, at the distance of centuries, the same grand confession, and rest not day and night saying,

> "Holy, Holy, Holy,
> The Lord God Almighty." (Revelation 4:8)

In the remarkable offerings of the Red Heifer, whose ashes, according to the Epistle to the Hebrews, pointed to the Most Holy Blood of Christ (Hebrews 9:13-14), as if to draw special attention to the divine majesty of its antitype, three ingredients were commanded to be consumed with the victim. The hyssop, which was one of them, was carefully chosen, and must have three branches; and, to challenge inquiry, the priest, as he flung each ingredient into the burning, exclaimed, Is this cedar? cedar? cedar? Is this hyssop? hyssop? hyssop? etc.; and so thrice in reference to each, to which the witnesses thrice replied, It is! it is! It is! (*See Numbers 19:1-10*)

And as if even this were not yet sufficient, the ashes themselves were divided into three portions and laid up in three holy places.

The fire taken from the Holy Altar for the daily offering of incense, as if to indicate to the thoughtful the Mystery of Prayer, as the joint act of Christ the Intercessor and man the supplicant, was first placed in a brazier containing four cabs (*2 Kings 6:25, An ancient measure, the eighteenth part of an ephah, or 2 and 5/6 of our corn measure*), and was then poured into a golden censer containing three. The seven golden lamps in the Candlestick, as if to utter the solemn lesson that the holy light they foreshadowed came from God to man, to reveal Him in the Church, are said to have been lighted alternately in groups of three and four. According to immemorial usage, the devout Jews wash three times before their morning prayers; in seven windings they place the phylacteries round their bare left arm, and in three round the second finger of their left hand, whereby they utter three promises as if addressed to them by each Person of the Holy Trinity:

"I will betroth thee unto Me forever:
I will betroth thee unto Me in righteousness, and in judgment,
And in lovingkindness, and in mercies:
I will even betroth thee unto Me in faithfulness,
And thou shalt know the Lord."

Three times they anciently offered, and still offer their daily prayers (Psalm 55:17, Daniel 6:10); three times three blasts of trumpets accompany their festive prayers on the Feast of Trumpets; three times they rest their dead on their way to the grave; three times they throw earth upon the coffin, whence probably our own sad custom; three times they cast earth or grass towards Heaven; three times they wash on their return from the graveyard; and three times the mourner sits down on his way to his bereaved home, and bows his head in prayer. It was endless to enumerate all instances in which they use the mystic three as referring to God or things Divine.

And the Scriptural usage of Four is analogous to the use of this number in heathen antiquity.

Space and time, the two great factors of material creation, are spoken of as four: there are four quarters of heaven, four corners of the earth; four winds sweep from the one, and four rivers breaking forth from Paradise irrigate the other. The four elements are also recognized; and there is an angel set over the fire, another over the water; four angels hold the winds; and the prince of demons has for a while usurped the dominion of the earth. The year, their great type of all time, is divided into four seasons, each day into four parts, and the night into four watches; and separated into four camps God's people lie round their mystic sanctuary. It is not difficult nor strange, then, that the number Four, when used in symbol, denoted man (the microcosm), or the Church, or the world (the macrocosm), in distinction from Deity.

Nor is this conclusion weakened when we attempt to read into meaning by it the peculiar form and shape of the three divisions of the Tabernacle. (*See the symbolical meaning of Seven, Note B.*)

It was within these divisions, as in enclosed spaces, that the sacrifices bled and were consumed, the holy incense rose, and the Ark was placed; and what then more obvious and simple than the suggestion that these four-square spaces foreshadowed the localities or spheres within which the Church must accomplish her several economies?

They all exhibited in form the cosmical number Four, but in marked diversity. Precisely as in a preceding part of this book the three divisions were shown to rise above each other in symbolical glory, and to attain their climax in the Most Holy; so, do these three enclosures rise above each other in regularity and symmetry, and attain perfection at the same termination.

The Court was one hundred cubits long, fifty cubits broad, and five high—its length, breadth, and height were thus diverse. The Holy Place was twenty cubits long, ten broad, and ten high—two of its measurements therefore were alike; but only the Most Holy was a perfect embodiment of the Four, and like the Heavenly City or Paradise in the Revelation, the Holy Place was a cube; or, as is said of the Heavenly City, the height and length and breadth of it were equal.

And if again we look from the type to the prototype, from the Tabernacle to the Church, we shall perceive the full meaning of this arrangement.

The Jewish Dispensation had its defined local sphere or habitation, namely the land of Palestine; and the enclosure which typified it, the Court, bore the cosmical hieroglyph, the number Four, embodied in its rectangular form.

The local sphere of the Christian Church, too, though she is called the Kingdom of Heaven, is here below—her field is the world.

Hence the Holy Place, the type of the Church's sphere, bore, like the other, the embodied Four in its four-square outlines.

But the appointed local habitation of the Church in glory also is on the earth.

> "Blessed are the meek,
> For they shall inherit the earth." (Matthew 5:5)
> "We look for a new heaven and new earth,
> Wherein dwelleth righteousness." (2 Peter 3:13)

"The righteous shall inherit the earth,
And shall dwell therein forever." (Psalm 37:29)

"Man, as a microcosm," says Olshausen (*in the Gospels, iii, p. 109*),

"appears as an emblem prefiguring every stage of development in the macrocosm; and just as it is only in the glorifying of the body that the development of an individual's life has its consummation, even so the glorifying agency of the Spirit reaches its climax only in the pervading of the material universe. This rich idea the Savior sets before His disciples, and . . . points them forward to this coming economy into which they shall one day visibly enter on its final manifestation."

Hence the enclosure of the Most Holy, also the section typical of this last locality, retained also the cosmical number or numerical hieroglyph, and was likewise four-square.

But when contrasted with the local sphere of Christianity, that of the Jewish economy was imperfect. Holy it was. They claimed a triple holiness for their land.

Highest was that of the Temple, then came the sanctity of Jerusalem, the holy city, then came that of their country, the holy land.

Physically perhaps, certainly morally, it was the glory of all lands. God dwelt there—Divine inspiration was there indigenous. Every inch of its soil was devoted to God, was held by the people as His stewards, and consecrated tenfold by the appearance of the Incarnate Lord.

"Out of Zion, the perfection of beauty,
God hath shined." (Psalm 1:2)
"The land which I had given them . . .
Which is the glory of all lands." (Ezekiel 20:6, 15)

> "The land shall not be sold for ever,
> For the *land is mine*,
> And ye are strangers, and sojourners with *me*."
> (Deuteronomy 25:23)

Yet the boundaries of Palestine were narrow, and though its holy influence travelled far beyond them, yet was that influence less extensive, and less revolutionizing than those of Christianity.

And another solemn change has come upon the material earth since Christ's death, which was accomplished not for Palestine merely, but for the whole world. His Holy Blood has touched the earth and has sanctified it. When:

> "He endured the shame and spitting
> Vinegar, and nails, and reed,
> As His blessed side is opened,
> Water thence and blood proceed;
> Earth, and sky, and stars, and ocean,
> By that flood are cleansed indeed."

In the garden of Gethsemane His blood fell upon the ground—in the judgment it flowed from His lacerated flesh, and, if an old tradition may be credited, stood there in pools: it fell from His head that was encircled with the crown of thorns, when He stood before Pilate and His accusers; it marked no doubt His weary footsteps to Calvary, flowed on His cross and upon the spot where it stood; flowed there afresh from the spear wound in His side, and most probably bedewed the grave where He lay.

Can anyone who feels something of the awful depth of this tremendous mystery believe in his heart that this sevenfold flowing of that blood upon the earth was accidental and undesigned? I cannot.

Nor is it at all difficult to read the meaning of this great fact. Had it not been carefully foreshadowed during fifteen hundred years in the Church? Not leprous persons merely, but leprous houses also, God commanded to be sprinkled seven times with sacrificial blood; and in both cases the very striking offering of two live birds, one of which was slain over running water, while the other, having been dipt in the warm blood of its fellow which had just been shed, was set free in the open field, was observed alike. And if the blood of the slain bird, when sprinkled on the leper, typified, as is confessed, the Holy Blood of Christ, is it not evident that the same blood, when sprinkled on the leprous house, did foreshadow the same great Antitype of all legal sacrifices? And if the leper was, as is also confessed, the type of sin-stricken man, what else could the leprous house have been intended to exhibit but man's sin-stricken habitation? "To teach us," says Bonar on Leviticus, "that this earth is under the curse, God sent the leprosy in houses; just as to teach that men are under the curse, He sent leprosy in their bodies."

And with deep truthfulness did the leprous house set forth the condition of our earth, for as the house itself could not have sinned, but was stricken for the sin of its inhabitant, so is this poor earth smitten on account of man's sin.

> "Cursed is the ground for thy sake." (Genesis 3:17)
> "The creature was made subject to vaity,
> Not willingly, or because it elected sin.
> And the same Holy God who subjected the earth to the curse,
> For us has subjected it in hope.
> Wherefore the creature itself also shall be delivered
> From the bondage of corruption
> Into the glorious liberty of the children of God."
> (Romans 8:20-21)

And by virtue of what else shall the curse be removed from the earth, but by that Blood which has taken away the curse from man. Verily the John the Baptist's words have a twofold meaning:

> "Behold the Lamb of God,
> Which taketh away the sins of the world." (John 1:29)

Christ's Blood has fallen 'upon the earth, the awful, mysterious Blood of the Incarnate, and has thus purchased and insured her final redemption.

Higher, then, and holier, is the condition of our very earth, or the local sphere which the Church occupies in this Dispensation than the sphere of the former; hence the Holy Place, the type of the economy, exhibited the cosmical Four in greater symmetry than the Court. But even this higher condition is but relative, not absolute.

The creature, or creation, says the apostle Paul, *shall* be set free—that is, unbound. The binding here implied, as it morally and judicially is the result of man's transgression, appears literally a physical fact, and continues to the present hour.

Of the sixty-five or sixty-six elements which modern science has discovered upon the earth, only four enter generally into active living combinations. The rest lie bound, and held in thralldom by an alien power. (*See Note C*)

And Nature waits the hour of the deliverance which the Blood of Christ has purchased for her.

The apostle Paul's words are very remarkable on this point. His language, in its strictly literal meaning, is as follows:

"As a redeemed captive listen with breathless and feverish attention for a promised signal when her chains shall fall, and her prison door shall be flung wide open, so waits Nature the signal of her restoration." (Romans 8:19)

How clearly loftier minds have apprehended the bondage of creation and her aspirations is beautifully expressed by Goethe. He says—

"When I stand all alone at night in open nature, I feel as though it were a spirit, and begged redemption of me. Often have I had the sensation, as if Nature, in wailing sadness, entreated something of me; so that not to understand what she longed for, out through my very heart."

The strife of the elements also continues, and the destruction of our globe is momentarily averted by a fearful and wonderful equipoise of forces. The interior of the earth, too, still is restless.

"Our repose," says Humboldt, "is but apparent, not real. The shocks which the surface of this earth experiences under every variety of climate . . . the gradual subsidence of continents, and the appearance of new eruptive islands, bear no testimony to quiescence within our globe."

"How precarious," says the author of *The Chemistry of Creation*, "is the position of the human family, when we remember those pent-up powers which are scarce restrained from tearing asunder . . . the crust on which we rest with such unthinking security. How entirely hopeless an attempt to escape, were it to please God to break the yoke which He has imposed on them, and to set them free."

But in the next Dispensation, partially at least at its commencement, and wholly after the thousand years, our earth and its encircling heavens shall be purified by fire, and freed from every vestige of corruption, shall return to all the glory she had before sin entered, or even more.

Hence our Bible, with a simplicity and majesty seldom reflected on, addresses to creation apostrophes such as these:

> "Let the sea roar,
> And the fulness thereof,
> The world, and they that dwell therein.
> Let the floods clap their hands,
> And let the hills be joyful together before the Lord,
> For He cometh...." (Psalm 97:7-9)

And the apostle John describes the grand swelling chorus of redeemed creation which he seems to have fore-heard on Patmos, when he says:

> "And every creature which is in heaven,
> And on the earth,
> And under the earth,
> And such as are in the sea,
> And all that are in them, heard I saying,
> Blessing, and honor, and glory, and power,
> Be unto Him that sitteth upon the throne,
> And unto the Lamb for ever and ever." (Revelation 5:13)

At the time of this high anthem, and then only, shall every trace of sin and sorrow have been obliterated from man and man's habitation forever and forever; and hence the last section of the Tabernacle, the type of the Church's local habitation in the next economy, still retained the cosmical signature in its form, but expressive of the highest symmetry and beauty—viz., the Four embodied in the cube—and in this respect, as in others, which I shall point out in a subsequent chapter, the Most Holy was the type of Jerusalem the Golden, of which the apostle John expressly informs us, that its length and breadth and height are equal.

NOTE A

St. Augustine says (*Tr. 27, s10*), on Christ's words, have not I chosen you twelve? "Twelve seems to be a sacred number, used in the case of those who were to spread the doctrine of the Holy Trinity through the four quarters of the globe." So also Bede.

On the number of the Apostles, in Matthew 10:2, Remigius, Archbishop of Rheims, 471, who baptized Clovis, king of the Franks, 496, says:

> "The number twelve is a perfect number, being made up of the number six, which has perfection because it is formed of its own parts, one, two, three, multiplied into one another; and the number six, when doubled, amounts to twelve."

On the draught of fishes numbering one hundred fifty and three, in John 21:11, St. Augustine says again (*Tr. 122*): "The number which signifies the law is ten, from the ten commandments. But when to the law grace is joined with the latter Spirit, the number seven is brought in, that being the number which represents the Holy Spirit, to whom sanctification properly belongs. For sanctification was first heard of in the Law, with respect to the seventh day; and Isaiah praises the Holy Spirit for His sevenfold work and office. The seven of the Spirit added to the ten of the Law, make seventeen; and the numbers from one to seventeen, when added together, make a hundred fifty and three. . . . . The number fifty is made up of seven sevens and one over, signifying that these sevens are one." So nearly also Greg. Horn. 24. (*Quoted from the Catena Aurea. Oxf. 1845.*)

On the number of the Beast, in Revelation 8:18, the Author of *Horae Apocalypticae* makes the following observations:

"It appears that it was a common custom, at the time of St. John, and indeed long before and long after, for three classes of persons to have certain Stigmata, or marks of appropriation, imprinted on them—viz., slaves, soldiers, and devotees of one or other god; that the impression was generally made on the forehead or hand, and that the mark was sometimes the simple name or characteristic emblem of the master or god, sometimes, as in the devotee's case, the god's particular hieroglyphic number . . . . (0.9., the number Three was sacred to Minerva, Four to Apollo).

"As to the inscription with a particular number as sacred, this was either some simple number consecrated to the devotee's god according to the Platonic or Pythagorean mysteries of numbers, or perhaps the number of letters in his name; or, as it might be, the number made up of the numeral values of the constituent letters of the name. Now it is evident that it is the last kind of number which is here intended as the number of the Beast."

Wordsworth says, on this mystic number:

"Seven is the number of completeness....It is rightly concluded that the seven Epistles to the seven churches are not to be regarded as inscribed only to them, but that they are the voice of the Holy Spirit to all the churches of Christendom to the end of time."

Vitringa:

"Seven is the number of Universality."

On Revelation 11:9, Wordsworth says again:

"The number three and a half, being the half of seven, represents a semi-perfect state—one of transition and probation, of spiritual toil, pilgrimage, and per section."

NOTE B

The Number Seven

I may perhaps mention here, in passing, that the ancients believed the number seven to be rightly called sacred, because it is the compound of three, the numerical symbol of God, and four, the numerical symbol of the world as a macrocosm, and man as its reflection, or the microcosm.

Thus Laur. Lydus, quoted by Bahr, to the latter of whom I am indebted for this thought, as well as some other thoughts developed in this volume,

> "Seven is composed of two most harmonious elements—viz., the three and four."

And this bisection of this number is found also in Holy Scripture. Thus, in reference to the purification of the ceremonially unclean, it was commanded that the third day and the fourth after the third—viz., the seventh—should be specially observed.

The words were as follows:

> "He that touched the dead body of any man
> Shall be unclean seven days.
> He shall purify himself with it on the third day,
> And on the seventh day
> He shall be clean." (Numbers 19:11-12)

And if he neglected the ritual of the third day, the seventh left him still unclean, and therefore, the law continues:

> "But if he purify not himself the third day,
> Then the seventh day
> He shall not be clean." (Numbers 19:12)

The same bisection is again commanded in the same chapter from which this passage is taken:

> "And for an unclean person
> They shall take of the ashes of the burnt heifer
> Of purification for sin,
> And running water shall be put thereto in a vessel:
> And a clean person shall take hyssop,
> And dip it in the water,
> And sprinkle it upon the tent,
> And upon all the vessels,
> And upon the persons that were there,
> And upon him that touched a bone,
> Or one slain, or one dead, or a grave:
> And the clean person shall sprinkle upon the unclean
> On the third day, and on the seventh day." (Numbers 19:17-19)

The same curious law is given for soldiers returning from battle, and their captives:

> "Abide without the camp seven days:
> Purify both yourselves and your captives on the third day,
> And on the seventh day." (Numbers 31:19)

A somewhat similar, if not more striking observance was commanded in the ritual for cleansing the leper. He must be marked with blood three times, and afterwards four times with holy oil, as follows:

> "And the priest shall take some of the blood . . .
> And put it upon the tip of the right ear
> Of him that is to be cleansed,
> And upon the thumb of his right hand,
> And upon the great toe of his right foot . . .
> And the priest shall take some of the log of oil,
> And pour it into the palm of his own left hand:
> And the priest shall dip his right finger
> In the oil that is in his left hand,
> And shall sprinkle of the oil with his finger
> Seven times before the Lord.
> And of the rest of the oil that is in his hand
> Shall the priest put upon the tip of the right ear
> Of him that is to be cleansed,
> And upon the thumb of his right hand,
> And upon the great toe of his right foot,
> Upon the blood of the trespass-offering:
> And the remnant of the oil that is in the priest's hand
> He shall pour upon the head of him that is to be cleansed."
> (Leviticus 14:14-18)

The ornaments on the candlestick exhibited an analogous arrangement, for the stem bore four groups of them, and each of the branches three; and Josephus says that they lighted alternately three and four of the lamps. (*Ant.* vi. 3, 9.)

"The same bisection of the seven," says Bengel, "is clearly observed in the seven churches, seven seals, seven trumpets, and seven vials of the

Revelation, and is at once clear, striking, and important." —*Einleit.* in d. *Offenb.* § 20.

If these various statements have weight, then it seems clear that the number seven, when symbolically used, denotes the union of God and man, or God and the world, as the case may be. On this supposition, the sprinkling of the sacrificial blood seven times may have symbolized the twofold fact of the union of the Divine and human natures in Him whom the legal sacrifice foreshadowed, and also the union or atonement between God and the penitent thereby effected. Sometimes this union or contact may have been one of judgment, as in the seven trumpet blasts which levelled the walls of Jericho before Israel's avenging host.

Remarkable is the fact that in this manner, too, the Tabernacle revealed itself at a glance to the tutored mind, as the place where God and man were united by its three divisions and its foursquare form—exhibiting at once the embodiment of the number Seven.

Perhaps the altars and other square forms may also have exhibited the seven in their three dimensions of length, breadth, and height, added to the four-square form.

NOTE C

"Nature," says Olshausen (*Com. on Rom. viii. 21*), "is bound by an alien power, and held in thralldom."

The author of *The Chemistry of Creation* acknowledges the same fact when he says:

> "The Creator has taken, as it were, a mere handful of elements, and has formed out of them not only the gorgeous structure on which we

dwell, but also ourselves—that is, our material bodies, and our fellow occupants of the earth, and the inhabitants of the air and the sea. . . . If, then, it has pleased God to rear this beautiful creation upon so small a comparative number of predominant elements; if it has pleased Him to show His glorious attributes of power and wisdom in the formation of such multifarious products out of, in the main, but a few materials, what powers of developing new and exquisite harmonies, fresh and yet more lovely combinations of matter than earth has ever beheld, does chemistry suggest to us, should it be consistent with His will, in the formation of a new heaven and earth, to call into more extensive use the elements which in the present plan take so comparatively an insignificant part in the work of creation! If, as we may be permitted to conjecture, out of such limited resources such an astonishing variety has been produced, what may not the beauty of creation he, should all the resources we know to exist be brought prominently into operation! If, to illustrate more clearly this idea, a great musician can produce charming music out of an instrument of but a few notes' compass, what soul-stirring melodies may we not expect when he is seated at a musical instrument better suited to display his powers!"

6

Symbolism of Sacred Vessels

The Way to Jerusalem the Golden Foreshadowed by the Sacred Vessels of the Court and of the Holy Place

On entering the Court of the Tabernacle, we stand, therefore, already on holy ground.

We are separated from an outlying world of sin, and breathe the atmosphere of God's habitation in His Church.

Nor is the entrance possible except through the Vail, the type, as we shall see below, of Christ—Christ uniting God and man in Himself.

For only in consequence of His eternal compassion by which He took flesh in predeterminate counsel before He actually assumed it, was the land of Israel consecrated to be the habitation of the Church.

Yet was this consecration of their land not enough to save the sinner in Israel. They imagine, indeed, that there is some saving virtue—even in the very soil of the Holy Land, and in all countries under heaven their devout members still purchase earth brought from Palestine, to place some of it under the heads of their dead.

But at the very entrance of the Court God commanded them to be admonished, that without personal holiness no man can be saved. This lesson was preached to them by the Brazen Laver.

THE HOLY PLACE

The Brazen Laver

In the water which it contained, the priests were commanded to wash their hands and feet before they entered upon their ministrations at the outer Altar, or in the Holy Place. If they neglected this injunction they must die.

But so far from disregarding it, their ablutions became more and more frequent, as time wore on.

In the Temple, where the Priests slept, who composed the course of priests on duty, they rose sometimes in the middle of the night and descended into a bath constructed for this purpose within the Sanctuary, where a lamp was always burning. Before *cock-crowing* all who were to act that day rose, and bathed, and the first words which the Captain of the Temple addressed to them as he entered were: "Let all that have performed their ablutions come forward and cast lots!"

Yet was not this sufficient—but when the officiating priest drew near the outer altar to take from it coals of fire, the other priests cried to him: "Touch no sacred vessel until thou hast sanctified thy hands and feet at the Laver!" (*Mid. c. l, M 1—4, incl.*) "Sanctified" was the word they used; for it was well understood that mere outward cleansing was useless, and that they needed inward purity.

And accordingly, Philo says (*De Vit. Mos.* ch. v. p. 521) that the devout women gave their mirrors for the construction of the Laver, that the Priests seeing themselves reflected on its polished surface, might pray for inward and spiritual purity; and their ancient tradition tells us that the water of the Laver denoted the tears of the penitent.

In this sense, the whole Church of Israel seems to have understood the lesson which the Laver was meant to teach when they sang:

> "I will wash mine hands in innocence;
> So, will I compass Thine Altar, O Lord!" (Psalm 26:6)

(*Scott has interpreted the first of these passages as follows: "By repentance and conscientious obedience, as well as by faith, expressed in attending on the typical purifications, the Psalmist prepared for offering those sacrifices which prefigured the atonement of Christ."*)

And again:

> "O send out Thy Light and Thy Truth:
> Let them lead me;
> Let them bring me unto Thy holy hill,
> And to Thy Tabernacles.
> Then will I go unto the Altar of God,
> Unto God my exceeding joy." (Psalm 43:3-4)

And I have no doubt that from the washing of the priests arose the habit of frequent ablutions among the Jews alluded to in the New Testament, and still so rigidly practiced by them. Most scrupulously do they wash before they offer their morning prayer, wherein they recount the ancient order of sacrifice, and hope that this prayerful remembrance will be accepted instead of it, since the destruction of the Temple, and their dispersion, renders the real offering impossible; and before they take their principal meals they wash also, for they consider them as sacramental, and precede them by partaking of bread and wine, which they bless.

Nor has the lesson of the Laver lost its meaning in Christianity. A divine atmosphere has been shed indeed upon all lands where Christianity has erected her banner, but we, too, require special personal grace.

Before we will come, and therefore practically before we can come, to Christ, we need His heavenly mind, not to, commend ourselves to Him, nor to venture near in conscious purity—No!

We say rightly:

Just as I am, without one plea,
But that Thy blood was shed for me,
And that Thou bidst me come to Thee,
O Lamb of God, I come!
Just as I am, and waiting not
To rid my soul of one dark blot;
To Thee, whose blood can cleanse each spot,
O Lamb of God, I come!

But then the disposition to seek Him out of personal need; the conviction that He is able and willing to pardon and to purify, whence are they?

Not of the human heart, but of God's grace; and yet these necessarily precede, were it but by the twinkling of an eye, our flight to Christ for participation in His Blood. Hence it is that the Fount, whose water typifies the first imparting of the Holy Ghost to the soul, stands within, but yet at the entrance of our churches. (*Founts . . . . were placed at first at some distance from the church; afterwards in the church porch, and that significantly, because Baptism is the entrance into the Church mystical. . . . . At last they were introduced in the church itself, being placed at the west end, near the south entrance." Hook's Church Dict., s. v. Fount.*)

But in very deed the Laver, as much as the Altar, is a type of Christ.

On the cross on which He died, He united both in Himself; for out of His blessed side proceeded both water and blood—water, the emblem of the Spirit which He bestows, and blood, that mysterious price of our redemption which the blood of legal offerings was intended to foreshadow.

The Brazen Altar, or Altar of Burn Offering

After the Laver stood the Brazen Altar, or The Altar of Burnt Offering. It received this name on account of the daily sacrifices which were offered upon it. (*Now this is that which thou shalt offer up on the altar; Two lambs of the first year day by day continually. The one lamb thou shalt offer in the morning; And the other lamb thou shalt offer at even. . .This shall be a continual burnt-offering throughout your generations. Exodus 29:38-39, 42*)

This is the law of the burnt-offering:

> "It is the burnt-offering, because of the burning upon the altar
> All night unto the morning,
> And the fire of the altar shall be burning in it . . .
> It shall not be put out:
> And the priest shall burn wood on it every morning,
> And lay the burnt-offering in order upon it . . .
> The fire shall ever be burning upon the altar;
> It shall never go out. (Leviticus 6:9, 12-13)

At dawn, the priests blew the trumpets, and, after sprinkling the blood, placed the morning sacrifice upon the fire on the altar, where it remained, its smoke rising up to Heaven until evening. And when the sun sank below the western horizon, a fresh blast of trumpets announced to the people that the evening sacrifice was about to replace the offering of the morning; and its smoke rose up to God all night.

This was the ancient practice, day by day, through years, and generations, and centuries. Thus was the Church, individually and collectively, preceded in the labors of the day, and silently overshadowed in their rest at night, by a sacrifice that pointed to Him whose mysterious life was yielded up in covenant before sin entered the world, and whose continuous and infinite merit causes the Divine showers of pardon, peace, and blessing, to descend day and night upon all the habitations of the Israel of God. And as the burning and smoking victim on the altar told the Church of the Savior, so also did the altar itself on which it lay.

The one clearly pointed to Him as man, the other as intelligibly, as God. I fear we underrate the apprehension of this great truth among the ancients.

Yet it is an instructive fact, that they called the altar by names which leave no doubt of their knowledge on this subject.

Thus, Jacob erected an altar at Shalem, "and called it El-elohe-Israel;" that is, God, the God of Israel. (Genesis 33:20) On what other possible ground can this awful name have been given, but that the Patriarch regarded the Altar as the symbol of his Redeemer's divinity?

Moses, who spoke with unmitigated scorn and uncompromising reprobation of the most distant approach to idolatry, must have had the same truth before him when he called an altar which he built, Jehovah-nissi, Jehovah my banner. (*Exodus 27:15*)

And so, perhaps with the growing clearness discernible in the march of Old Testament revelation, Ezekiel called the altar he sees in vision, the Lion of God, an unmistakeable name of our Lord. (*Ezekiel 43:15-16 in the original.*) (*See Note A*)

The explanation of these remarkable designations obviously is, that as the sacrifices upon the fires of the altar adumbrated the Lord's Humanity, so did the altar itself point to His Divine nature. (*See Note B*)

And this view is supported by our Lord Himself, when He says that the altar is greater than the sacrifice. Both sacrifice and altar were but shadows, and derived their importance wholly from the reality to which they referred. But as a shadow of Christ's Sacrifice, the importance of the legal victims was immeasurable; and yet our Lord says the greatness to which the altar pointed transcends it. Then lies not the thought very near, that the altar pointed to His Divinity?

And still further is this conclusion justifiable by the additional saying of our Lord, that the altar sanctifies the sacrifice for was it not the union of His Divine with His Human nature which imparted to the latter its majesty inconceivable, and to His Sacrifice its miraculous and eternal efficacy? (*See Notes C and D*)

The following most important lessons seem to me to have been foreshadowed by this altar:

First

To the beholder it seemed to be of solid brass; the eye could detect nothing else upon the most searching inspection. Yet, by express Divine command, it concealed between its outer and inner brazen surfaces, and protected from the Divine fire that consumed the superincumbent victim, a pleroma, or "fulness," of imperishable wood.

This feature is so prominently stated, and recurs again in other sacred vessels, that a distinct notice of it cannot subject me to the charge of trifling. The key to this mystery lies near.

Wood and tree are synonymous in the original language of the Old Testament (e. g. *The cherubim of Solomon are said to have been made of olive-tree. 1 Kings vi. 23*) and imperishable trees are so frequently spoken of as emblems of God's saints, that the thought is readily suggested that this pleroma or fulness of the altar foreshadowed Christ's members—the pleroma, or "fulness of Him that filleth all in all." (Ephesians 1:23)(*See Note E*)

It was a visible parable of the mystical union between Christ and His people. As the wood was hidden within the altar, so in God's eye were they hid in Him; and as the fire of God descended on the victim that lay upon the altar, but could not reach the wood, so has the fearful punishment of sin fallen upon the Church's Sacrifice. Yet she herself is most safe, because in Christ; and

> "There is therefore now no condemnation
> To those which are in Christ Jesus." (Romans 8:1)

Second

The altar upbore the sacrifice enabled the fire of God to search it through, until that fire was satisfied and abated—even as His eternal Spirit up-bore and sustained His humanity while He endured that great death; or, as the apostle Paul has it,

> "He through the Eternal Spirit
> Offered Himself *perfectly* to God." (Hebrews 9:14)

(The Greek word *amomos* is the equivalent for the Hebrew *tamim*, and means *perfect* as well as immaculate, both in a physical and moral sense. See Fuerst. *Concord. Heb.* s. v.) (*See Note F*)

On the other hand, the fire that consumed the sacrifice heated the brass on the altar, though it could not melt it, as if to show the sympathy of the Divine with the sufferings of the human nature, and the blood of the Atonement was poured upon the altar (Deuteronomy 12:17), until the altar itself appeared as a blood-deluged sacrifice.

God forbid—I write this thoughtfully and solemnly—that I should venture into too curious thoughts on this mightiest of mysteries; but I cannot help reflecting, in this connecton, on the remarkable analogy between this type of Christ and some of the profoundest passages in the Epistles of Paul.

Thus, the Apostle hints the sympathy between the Godhead and Manhood of our Lord in the act of His death, when he says:

> "Feed the Church of God,
> Which He hath purchased with His own Blood." (Acts 20:28)

I am aware that some read it the Church of the Lord; but what of that? Is not our Lord very God and very man?

Besides, the best authorities read as our translators did.

Third

But still more clearly and explicitly is the death of our Lord spoken of as the death of His Church, as though she had participated in it and had died with Him. The apostle Paul says again:

> "We thus judge,
> That if One died for all,
> Then all died"—or, as our version gives it—
> "then were all dead." (2 Corinthians 5:14)

Those, then, that are in Christ, as the imperishable wood was in the altar, are viewed as if a judicial and atoning death had passed on themselves, and had set them free.

Fourth

In Christ alone souls are safe; out of Christ God is a consuming fire.

But why should anyone be out of Christ?

The Altar was surmounted by four horns, the well-known emblems of power; and these horns were deeply marked with Sacrificial blood; and it fell from them as it fell from Him whom the Altar typified, in the garden and on the Cross.

These horns were therefore at once symbols of might and reconciliation, and were outstretched to the four corners of the earth, to call all men to flee unto Christ to be saved.

These exalted facts in Redemption are assuredly not unworthy of the care with which God ordered their typical representation; and by these embodiments of Truth, in connectons of course with instruction by God's appointed teachers, were the ancients prepared for the next and higher facts to be revealed to the Church in the second, the Christian Dispensation, set forth in the vessels of the Holy Place.

Before we enter on the contemplation of these vessels, I venture to call attention to the Vail which concealed them from the Court.

The Vail of the Holy Place

According to the Holy Scripture, the Vail was a type of Christ; and when His holy flesh was torn and rent upon the Cross, its type, "the Vail of the Temple, was rent in twain from the top to the bottom." (Matthew 27:51) (*See Note G*)

To this Paul alludes when he speaks, in the passage quoted in the note, of the new and living way which the Savior has opened for us through the Vail—that is, His Flesh. It points, then, chiefly to His human nature; but as that is inseparably united with His Divine, the Vail exhibits distinct traces of both. The basis of the Vail was fine white linen, the emblem of sinless purity, as it is written:

> "Come now, and let us reason together,
> Saith the Lord:

> Though your sins be as scarlet,
> They shall be as white as snow;
> Though they be red like crimson,
> They shall be as wool." (Isaiah 1:18)

In the same sense we are told—

> "Many shall be purified, and made white." (Daniel 12:10)
> "And some of them of understanding shall fall,
> To try them, and to purge,
> And to make them white." (Daniel 11:35)

And again—

> "The marriage of the Lamb is come,
> And His bride hath made herself ready.
> And to her was granted
> That she should be arrayed in fine linen,
> White and clean;
> For the fine linen is the righteousness of the saints."
> (Revelation 19:7-8)(*See Note H*)

The Vail pointed thus to the ineffable Purity which belongs to Him at once as the Holy One of Israel, and the Man Christ Jesus, who was holy, harmless, undefiled, and separate from sinners.

But it was also embroidered with crimson, blue, and purple.

In Holy Scripture blood is said to be life (Deuteronomy 22:23) and man to be born of blood. (John 1:13)

But blood is red or crimson; hence this color when used symbolically seems clearly to be an emblem of man, or humanity. And this conclusion is still further supported by the fact that the generic appellation of Scripture for man is Adam, which signifies red, blood, and man. (*See Gesen. Thes. s. v. Dam. p. 27. The Greek also signifies both man in contrast with the immortal gods, and blood. Od. v. 5341.*)

The crimson part of the embroidery in the Vail pointed, it would seem, to our Lord as man—the second Adam.

Blue is the color of the Heavens, which we connect instinctively with the Seat and Temple of God. Even our blessed Lord lifted up His eyes to heaven in prayer (John 17:1), and Stephen the Martyr:

> "*Looked up* steadfastly into heaven,
> And saw the Glory of God." (Acts 7:55)

Blue was therefore a natural symbol of heaven, and by an easy transition of thought, of God also, both among the Jews and among the heathen.

The Egyptians painted the images of some of their gods blue, and the Persian sofi wore blue mantles, to signify that they aspired to a Divine life, and were engaged in the study and contemplation of Divine mysteries.

In Christian art this color is usually employed to symbolize Divine attributes, or perfections.

All the male members of the Church of Israel were commanded to put a ribband or border of blue upon their four-fringed sacred vestments—

> "That they might look upon it,
> And remember.
> And do all God's commandments
> And be holy unto their God." (Numbers 15:37-40)

The blue marked them as Divine, and was to remind them of their duty to be like God.

This border of their garments the hypocritical Pharisees enlarged, and the Lord rebuked them for it, inasmuch as their lives were unlike the pretension which the broad border was clearly intended to declare. (*See Note I*)

Blue is moreover directly associated in the Scriptures with the true heavens and the throne of God, as when, for instance,

> "Moses, Aaron, Nadab, and Abihu,
> And the seventy elders of Israel,
> Saw the God of Israel:
> And under His feet
> As it were a paved work of sapphire stone,
> Even the substance of heaven in its splendor." (Exodus 24:9-10)

Or when the Prophet Ezekiel saw

> "Above the firmament
> The likeness of a throne,
> As the appearance of a sapphire stone." (Ezekiel 1:2)

The deep celestial blue on the Vail seems then to have been a well-known symbol of His Divinity whom the Vail foreshadowed.

The purple—or purpura clarissima, as the purple of the Tabernacle has been called—is the compound of scarlet and blue, and appears to have foreshadowed the hypostatical union—i.e. the union of the Divine and human natures in the Person of our Lord.

It would seem to have been selected to reveal the intimacy and perfection of this union; and the constituent colors of purple, red, and blue, to have been set in juxtaposition with it, to teach that although the two natures are thus combined in Him, yet are they not absorbed in each other, as if the Divine had been lost in the human, or the human in the Divine, but ever remain to coexist, notwithstanding their most perfect union. (*See Note J*)

And this mystic Vail, marked with red, and blue, and purple, was rent in twain from the top to the bottom when its Great Anti-type, the Lord, was pierced and His Holy Flesh was rent upon the Cross.

Once more the grand type uttered the fact inculcated before in the blood-stained Altar and its superincumbent sacrifice; but this time with still deeper and more awful suggestions.

And now, after this Vail was torn asunder, and, to use the language of Origen (p. 184), "the mysteries were published which had been concealed before with good reason," the Church entered upon her second and higher Dispensation.

The Laver and the Altar typified the characteristic prerogatives of the Jewish economy; beyond them their spiritual vision penetrated not with any degree of clearness. And how few, at least at the close of their polity, comprehended the meaning of the mysteries of the Court, is painfully evident from the reluctance with which even the Apostles admitted the need of Christ's vicarious sufferings and death. Of the power of His Intercession, taught by the Altar of Incense, they seem to have known nothing, and hence there grew up among them about that time, at all events only since their return from Babylon, the habit of praying to the dead. (*See Note K*)

The first sacred vessel that met the eye of the priest entering the Holy Place was

The Golden Altar or Altar of Incense

It was also called the Altar of Incense, was smaller than the outer altar, was made of wood and metal like the other; but, unlike it, was overlaid with fine gold instead of brass.

This costlier metal clearly indicated that He whom the altar symbolized had entered upon a higher state than that in which He appeared before—in the Court, the type of the Jewish economy.

That was the period of His profound humiliation; but when He had fulfilled the typical prophecy of the brazen altar, and had died for our offenses, He entered into His state of exaltation.

Precisely the same great fact was again pointed out by the pure golden crown which surmounted this Golden Altar, and still further distinguished it from the uncrowned Altar of the Court.

> "We see Jesus,
> Who was made a little lower than the angels,
> For the suffering of death,
> Crowned with glory and honor." (Hebrews 2:9)

The Golden Altar suggests the following lessons:

First

The sweet Incense which was offered upon it continually was the emblem of the Lord's Intercession for His people.

At the time of the daily morning sacrifice one of the priests on duty took holy fire from the outer Altar, placed it in a golden brazier, and carried into the Holy Place, where a second priest received it. The priest who had brought it in fell on his face, and retired. Another priest carried a golden vial full of incense, placed Within a golden censer, into the Holy Place, fell also on his face, and retired.

The sound of a bell announced to the people in the Court that it was the time of incense, and of prayer. (Luke 1:8-10)

A third priest now poured out the fire on the Golden Altar: and a fourth took the vial of incense from the censer, and gave it to the priest whose lot it was to burn it "before the Lord." It had been observed that, as the Lord had blessed the house of Obed Edom, while the Ark was there, so a peculiar blessing attended the priest who offered incense; and it therefore became a law that no priest should perform the service more than once in his life (*Iom.* c. 2, sect. 4; *Tamid.* cc. 6, 7.)

The smoke of the incense rose from the Altar perpetually, and probably rolled through the open network which was above the Vail of the Most Holy in the Temple, where it blended with the Cloud of Glory that rested over the Mercy Seat.

Incense was an emblem of prayer (Revelation 5:8; Psalm . v. 8; Psalm 151:2); and we see here, as in a mirror, the great blessing of praying through Christ; for the inner Altar, like the outer, symbolized the Lord and His Church, and the incense upon it therefore foreshadowed the joint offering of the Savior and His people.

In this manner the apostle John appears to have seen it in vision, when he says:

> "The four living creatures (Cherubim),
> And four and twenty elders,
> Fell down before the Lamb,
> Having every one of them . . .
> Golden vials full of incense (not odours),
> Which are the prayers of the saints . . .

> And I saw ...
> And another angel (Christ comp. 1 Timothy 2:5)
> Came and stood at the altar,
> Having a golden censer:
> And there was given unto Him
> Much incense (comp John 5:26; 3:27),
> That he should offer it *with* the prayers of all saints
> Upon the golden altar
> Which was before the throne,
> And the smoke of the incense,
> With the prayers of the saints
> Ascended up before God
> Out of the angel's hand." (Revelation 5:8; 8:3-4)

No one was permitted to imitate that incense and offer it at home, or anywhere except on the Golden Altar; for no prayer is acceptable unless it is offered in and by our Lord; but when a soul has complied with these Divine conditions, her earnest prayers partake of His Omnipotence.

Second

The horns of the Altar, like the horns of the outer Altar, were tipped with the blood of the sin-offering, as it is written:

> "And the priest shall dip his finger in the blood,
> And sprinkle of the blood seven times
> Before the Lord,
> Before the Vail of the Sanctuary.
> And the priest shall put some of the blood
> Upon the horns of the Altar of Sweet Incense
> Before the Lord." (Leviticus 4:3, 6, 7)

His omnipotence and the merits of His Sacrifice overshadow His saints whilst they plead in Him, and He pleads for them.

Third

The Altar stood in the Holy Place, the type of the Church's local habitation. Our Lord is gone into the heavens and sat down on the right hand of Power. That Session is foreshadowed with wonderful precision by the Mercy Seat (see below). Yet the same Lord who, when in humiliation on earth, could speak of Himself as being at the same time in heaven, can now in His exaltation, though in heaven, be also upon earth.

And He is on earth, for He promised,

> "Where two or three are gathered together
> In my name,
> There am I in the midst of them." (Matthew 18:20)

Nay, He is with every one of His saints perpetually, for He said again:

> "Lo! I am with you always,
> Even to the end of the world," (Matthew 28:20)

and the Christian may therefore pray most trustfully—

> Abide with me from morn till eve,
> For without Thee I cannot live;
> Abide with me when night is nigh,
> For without Thee I dare not die.

Everywhere He is the Golden Altar of His people, and the praying Christian is overshadowed by His might and merits.

The Golden Candlestick

Nearer the Vail of the Most Holy, on the south side of the Holy Place, stood the Golden Candlestick. It was made of a talent of fine gold, rose from a triple root; and its shaft or stem and seven branches were marked by trinal mystic ornaments, the signature of Deity.

Its fiery seven lamps signified, it should seem, the seven Spirits of God, for the apostle John, when he saw them in holy vision, said:

> "Out of the throne proceeded lightnings,
> And thundering's, and voices;
> And there were seven lamps of fire
> Burning before the throne,
> Which are the Seven Spirits of God." (Revelation 4:5)

Every other sacred vessel in this mystic house of God represents the Lord Jesus, and the candlestick appears to foreshadow Him, shedding forth the sevenfold Spirit of God upon the Church.

Nor is this mere inference. For again the apostle John sees the Seven Spirits, but now they are most intimately associated with the Lord. He says:

> "And I beheld,
> And lo! in the midst of the throne,
> And of the four Cherubim,
> And in the midst of the twenty-four elders,
> Stood a Lamb, as it had been slain,
> Having seven horns,
> And [having] seven eyes,
> Which are the Seven Spirits of God." (Revelation 5:6)

And because the Holy Ghost reveals Himself in the Church, and is reflected by her, John sees the Lord Jesus again as the divine Root and Stem of the candlestick in the midst of the seven lamps (not candlesticks) which are the seven Churches, i. e. as we have seen before, the Church universal. (Revelation 1:12; 13-20)

This sacred vessel was, therefore, the type of the Savior, giving the fulness of His Spirit to His people.

It appears the visible exhibition of these words:

> "It is expedient for you
> That I go away;
> For if I go not away
> The Comforter will not come unto you;
> But if I depart
> I will send Him unto you." (1 John 16:7)
> "This Jesus hath God raised up,
> Whereof we all are witnesses.
> Therefore, being by the Right Hand of
> God exalted,
> And having received of the Father the promise of the Holy Ghost,
> He hath shed forth this,
> Which ye now see and hear." (Acts 2:32-41)

The most obvious practical lessons which the Golden Candlestick suggests are these:

First

In our higher dispensation, the glorious dawn of the Kingdom of Heaven, we walk no longer by the half divine, half earthly light of the Court, or the Jewish economy. Then, the Holy Ghost was not yet given, for Jesus was not yet glorified. Hence, their need of extraordinary

Divine messengers, the Holy Prophets, which in some degree made up the economic deficiency; and hence, also, the frequent, striking interposition of God. But now the Church is left without these collateral aids; for she has received, and is commanded and encouraged to walk in, His sevenfold light—a light not to be confounded on any account with frigid starlight of mere theological science—but which at once penetrates the soul, reveals in it and to it with ever growing splendor the perfect work of Jesus, and purifies the whole complexion of our intellectual and moral being.

Second

But, solemn warning! the very existence of this light, as well as the degree of its intensity, is dependent on the vigilance of the priest—of each individual soul. The Church helps you—but you yourselves must late and early tend that divine light, or fire; but if you are careless, the lamp of God in you may burn mournfully low, or be extinguished. Hence, the solemn admonition comes to all of us:

"Quench not the Spirit." (1 Thessalonians 5:19)

And also, the other cheering exhortation:

"Be ye filled with the Spirit!" (Ephesians 5:18)

How pure, and clear, and heavenly, ought to be the life of all who bear the name of Christian!

The lower degree in which the Holy Ghost was given in the bygone dispensation of the Church was typified by the Laver.

It, too, denoted the gift of the Holy Spirit, miraculous and blessed indeed, but in a comparatively feebler grade. In this feebler degree He is pledged to us in the Sacrament of Baptism; but the Church, with her supernatural instincts, has taught her baptized members to seek the higher in the rite of Confirmation. Hence the Office for that rite contained that ancient prayer, which, from the earliest times, has been used in all the Western Churches: "Almighty and everlasting God, who hast vouchsafed to regenerate these Thy servants by water, and the Holy Ghost, and hast given unto them forgiveness of all their sins, pour into them Thy sevenfold Spirit, the Holy Comforter from Heaven."

The Table of Shewbread

The Golden Table stood on the north side of the Holy Place opposite the Golden Candlestick, and on it were placed the twelve loaves of Shewbread.

First

The Shewbread bore the same relation to the holy table as the sacrifice to the brazen altar, the incense to the golden censer, and the seven burning lamps to the candlestick.

As in the Court the Lord is symbolized as offering Himself for the sins of the world, and in the Holy Place perpetually pleading for His people, and shedding down upon them His sevenfold Spirit, so on the twice-crowned table He is foreshadowed the source and sustenance of their higher Spirit-life, which enables them to receive, to retain, and to develop it.

Second

The name which the Scriptures give to this bread we have translated Shewbread, in imitation of Luther's rendering. But the original word means literally "the bread of the face," an entirely idiomatic form, and like the expression, "The angel of the face" who saves Israel. (Isaiah 63:9)

But the Savior of Israel, and therefore the Angel of the Face, is the Son of God, who is called again simply the Face of God, in Exodus 33:14, where it is said, "My Face shall go with thee, and I will give thee rest." (*orig*)

He is called the Face of God, in the same manner as the Word of God, for He reveals God; and especially because, as the human face in its normal condition, before it is dimmed and darkened by sin and sorrow and age, forms the clear index of the unseen Spirit within, the Lord so faithfully reveals the Father that He is called His express image, and says Himself,

> "He that hath seen Me
> Hath seen the Father." (John 14:9)

The bread of the face is therefore but an esoteric, secret appellation for the Bread of God, as which He plainly reveals Himself in the greater clearness of the New Testament, when He says:

> "The Bread of God is He
> Which cometh down from heaven,
> And giveth life to the world." (John 6:33)

Other collateral facts connected with the Shewbread point to the same conclusion. Thus the flour of which it was made was the perpetual gift of the children of Israel, as the water which was combined with it (for it consisted only of wonderfully refined flour, and water) was the gift of Heaven; and we know that the Savior, as touching His manhood, came of Israel, and was the glorious gift of that people to the world, a gift which every Jewish mother coveted and hoped to bestow.

And this purest bread was renewed scrupulously every Sabbath, and was therefore always fresh. But fresh, in this sense, is in Scripture phraseology synonymous with living: thus, fresh water, in opposition to stagnant or dead, is very often called living water. This Shewbread was therefore living bread; and the Lord Himself says,

"I am the Living Bread." (John 6:51)

And again, the unconscious and undersigned testimony of the Hebrew Fathers confirms my statement.

For the bread, they say, was pierced, as the Lord was pierced; it was anointed, too, with oil, in the form of a cross, and possessed a miraculous nutritive power. (See Toma, xliii. 3; lxxx. l. M. Menach. xi.)

It was also called Holy of Holies, and eaten only by the priests within the Sanctuary, since those only whom the ancient priests typified, viz., the true members of Christ in this higher economy, are called to eat the Bread of God while they abide in their high vocation; and these only will find it a heavenly nutriment; others may presume and affect to eat it, but it will turn to judgment.

Third

But the Shewbread was evidently also a type of Christ's people, exactly as we have seen the Incense to apply both to the Lord and His members, and the Seven Lamps to be the fulness of the Spirit proceeding from Christ, and reflected in His Church.

The Shewbread consisted of twelve loaves, and was thus the memorial of the twelve tribes of Israel, and perhaps by anticipation the emblem of the Apostles, the founders of the Christian church. The reason why Christ and His people should be symbolized here by the same material substance seems to me twofold.

First, because the spiritual food we receive transforms us into its own nature. As Paul writes:

> "The cup of blessing which we bless,
> Is it not the participation of the blood of Christ?
> The bread which we break,
> Is it not the participation of the body of Christ
> For we, the many, are one bread, ...
> For we are all partakers of that one bread."
> (1 Corinthians 10:16-17)

The word participation, which I substitute in this passage for the word communion in our English version, is used by Alford. And he says this strong literal sense must here be held fast, as constituting the very kernel of the Apostle's argument.

> "The wine is Me *Blood, the bread* is the *Body of Christ*. . . .We receive into us, make by assimilation part of ourselves, that wine, that bread; we become, therefore, by participation of that bread, one bread—i. e. one body; hence the close and literal participation in and with Christ. If we are to render this is, represents, or symbolizes, the argument is made void. On the other hand it is painful to allude to, though necessary to reprobate . . . the gross materialism of transubstantiation." (Com. l. c.)

But, secondly, the Shewbread points out the members of Christ, because they spend themselves, and are spent for others; so that others are quickened and strengthened by them. "In the same manner," says Olshausen, "as Christ calls Himself the bread that came down from Heaven, so is the Church collectively the representative of Christ, and the bread of life for the whole world."

Fourth

But the Golden Table and its holy burden stood close to the Vail of the Most Holy, and was seen only by the light that fell from the seven lamps of the Golden Candlestick. Then, by the example of Nadab and Abihu, let men beware of bringing common light to look on the "Tremendous Table," as the ancients called it; and let them also very distinctly understand that the clearness with which the Table and Bread were apprehended depended entirely on the degree of illumination derived from the mystic lamps.

If the Holy Ghost shines clearly in your soul, you will know much of the Christian's Bread of Life.

Thus, then do the vessels of the Holy Place utter in symbolism the great distinctive features of the Christian dispensation.

The mysteries shadowed forth in the Court are still full of force, and of the most vital importance.

They point out the first steps in our way to the golden city, and are indispensable.

It is God's way, and we may not depart from it; and every member of Christ's Church has, as it were, to come to the Court—but he must not tarry there, but *pass on* to the higher mysteries of the Holy Place.

The Court contains only the first elements of our religion, or, as the apostle Paul also calls them, milk for babes. He makes use of both expressions when he says:

> "Ye have need
> That one teaches you again which be the first principles
> (literally, the alphabet)
> Of the oracles of God;
> And are become such as have need of milk,
> And not of strong meat.
> For every one that used literally, that keeps on using milk

Is unskillful in the word of righteousness;
For he is a babe." (Hebrews 5:12-13)

And he describes as purely elementary, or as milk for babes, the very realities foreshadowed in the Court by the Laver and the Altar when he imperatively exhorts us to leave the alphabet of the doctrine of Christ, and to go on unto perfection,

"Not laying again the foundation of repentance
From dead works,
And faith toward God,
Of the doctrine of baptisms . . .
And of laying on of hands." (Hebrews 6:1-2)

Alas! how thankful are Christ's ministers in these days of the Church's ease, if they can lead their congregations and parishes even to the belief of the rudiments of Christianity! ("That word, or discourse, which has respect to the fundamental and elementary things mentioned below— let us press on to maturity."—*Alford*, l. c.)

But neither in nature nor in grace is a being that ever remains a babe a happy object.

Though it be your own child, it is but a sickly, dwarfed thing, and fulfils not its mission in your house or country. It was first a thing of joy and tender care, but is now a source of grief and disappointment; and if it were possible that its growth were hindered by its own obstinacy and resolute disobedience, would it not be much worse?

"The doctrine of laying on of hands . . . not being confined to any one special rite, will mean the reference and import of all that imposition of hands which was practiced under the law. . ." Alford, Z. c. It was specially practiced in offering sacrifices.

And is it not most ominous that, somehow, the apostle Paul couples the determination in professing Christians to remain babes, with apostasy?

He first chides them for remaining infants—then exhorts them to advance, and adds as in threatening:

> "For it is impossible for those
> Who were once enlightened
> And have tasted (mark, carefully and prayerfully!
> Have tasted, but not drunk deep,)
> Of the heavenly gift . . .
> If they shall fall away,
> To renew them again unto repentance."

(Until the Reformation, this was uniformly interpreted of God's grace given in Baptism."—Alford, l. c.)

The old Latin version renders the words, not *laying again the foundation* of repentance, by "non iterum fundamenta diruentes"—that is, not again destroying the foundation of repentance, &c.

This is not the literal meaning of the words, but that rendering shows us how the ancient Church felt that to turn perpetually on the first doctrines of Christianity, as a door on its hinges, is to perish. And is not this analogous to that most solemn warning given by Christ Himself, in Matthew 7:43?

When the unclean spirit is gone out of a man—clearly, the unclean spirit goes out of no man but by the operation of the Holy Ghost; and he, the subject of this beginning of the Divine life in him, instead of seeking the plenitude of His light and life, is *practically* satisfied with what he has attained, the result is that an utter emptiness of real faith and spirituality succeeds, which prepares him for that second fearful invasion of the evil one, which is indeed worse than the first. *(Alford on Matthew 4:3; see also Luke 11:24. Rabanus says (Catena Aurea, l. c.): "For when any one is converted to the faith, the devil is cast out of him in Baptism, who, driven thence, wanders up and down through dry places, that is, the hearts of the faithful, where he can find no rest. And returning to his house whence he has gone out, he findeth it empty of good works through slothfulness, and swept, that is, of its old vices, by baptism, and garnished with feigned virtues through hypocrisy... ")*

Is not this chain of thought in the inspired apostle alarming! Is not a carelessness about progress in spiritual life stagnation, and is not that a state of spiritual coma—the ominous precursor of ruin? And does not our choice seem to lie between advance to the Seven Spirits of God, and that retrogression which makes the soul the house of seven demons?

Can it be safe, or wise, to halt and balance between the two?

And can such halting and balancing end in Jerusalem the Golden?

Should we not rather most thankfully pursue our holy course in God's own appointed way?

And now we stand once more before the Vail of the Most Holy Place. Within its types are accumulated that reveal it as the representative of the Heavenly Jerusalem. I shall venture to enumerate a few of these.

Note A

In Isaiah 19:1, Jerusalem also is called Ariel, the Lion of God, but the Rabbins expressly refer this to the Temple (which as a whole is also a type of our Lord) in middot, c. 1 § 7. "The Temple was broad in front, but smaller in the rear, and thus resembled a lion in shape, as it is written: Ho! Lion of God, Lion of God, the city of David's camp;" but Buxtorf (Hist. Ign. Sacr. 2) understands it to have been said of the altar, by synecdoche.

Note B

If it be objected that the Jews were forbidden to make to themselves any graven image, or the likeness of anything in heaven or in earth, and, least of all, similitudes of God, I reply:

1. God Himself commanded Solomon, through his father David, to represent lions, oxen, palm trees, and flowers, in the Temple, which were similitudes of things on earth: hence the commandment prohibited only images of things earthly of man's device, but not those which God Himself commanded.
2. If this is incontrovertible in reference to images of things on earth prohibited in the second commandment, there is no reason why the permission should not extend also to images of things in heaven when made after the will of G

Note C

The Greek "doron," which our translators have chosen to render "gift" in the passage referred to, is the equivalent of the Hebrew "corban," the name for sacrifice in general use throughout Leviticus and Numbers.

Note D

Archdeacon Law, in his book, *Christ is All*, speaks of the altar as the type of the Lord's Divinity, as follows:

> "On what altar can Christ place Himself... This holy victim bears the countless sins of countless multitudes. What can support Him when the avenging fire falls? ... The help of worlds would crumble into dust." ... Christ alone can now uphold Himself. His Deity alone can keep humanity uncrushed. Christ's only altar is Himself."

He also recognizes in these words the animal victim as the type of the Lord's humanity, but he misses the truth when he speaks of the wood in the altar as being another type of His human nature.

Note E

"The righteous shall be like a tree
By the rivers of waters,
That bringeth forth his fruit in his season;
His leaf also shall not wither. . . . ." (Psalm 1:1-2)

The Church of Israel is:

"As trees of lign aloes
Which the Lord hath planted,
And as cedars beside the waters." (Numbers 24:5-6)

And the individual saint:

"As a tree planted by the waters,
That spreadiest out her roots by the river,
And shall not see when heat cometh,
But her leaf shall be green;
And she shall not be careful in the year of drought,
Neither shall cease from yielding fruit." (Jeremiah 17:8)

Again, it is said:

"I will be as the dew unto Israel:
He shall grow as the lily,
And cast forth his roots as Lebanon.
His branches shall spread,

And his beauty shall be as the olive tree,
And his smell as Lebanon.
They that dwell under his shadow shall return."
(Hosea 14:57)

Thus, was the Church compared to imperishable wood, or an imperishable tree.

Note F

The remarks of Ebrard and Alford on this passage are very important.

"The sacrifice of Christ could only be offered in the power of eternal spirit. Only that eternal spirit of absolute love, holiness, wisdom, and compassion was capable of enduring that sacrificial Death. . . This verse is, in a practical view, one of the most important in the whole New Testament. . . For as directed against the doctrine here taught concerning the value of Christ's sacrifice, all that calumnious talk of Rationalists and new German Catholics about a theology of blood and wounds, and a tyrannical God, who 'would look only on blood,' is put to a shameful silence. The main thing in the sacrifice of Christ . . . is that eternal spirit of absolute eternal holiness and eternal love which has efficaciously manifested itself in time, inasmuch as it endured the real bloody death for the sinful World."—Ebrard, *l.c.*

"Christ offered Himself with His own consent, assisting and empowering the sacrifice. And what was that consent? the consent of what? Of the spirit of a man? . . . No; . . . the Divine Spirit of His Godhead . . . was the agent in the offering, penetrating and acting on the humanity." *Alford, ibid.*

Note G

"Having therefore, brethren,
Liberty of access into the Holy Places
In the blood of Christ,
By a new and living way,
Which He hath consecrated for us
Through the Vail,
That is to say, His *flesh*." (Hebrews 10:19-20)

There is a very general impression that the Vail rent at the moment when the Lord yielded up the ghost (Matthew 27:51) was the inner Vail, which concealed the Most Holy. But this is mere arbitrary conjecture. In the early Church it was not the general opinion. Origen says: "It is understood that there were two Vails; one vailing the Holy of Holies, the other the outer part of the Tabernacle or Temple. In the passion, then, of our Lord and Savior, it was the outer Vail which was rent from the top to the bottom; that by rending of the Vail . . . the mysteries might be published which were concealed with good reason until the Lord's coming. But when that which is perfect is come, then the second Vail also shall be taken away, that we may see the things that are hidden within, to wit, the True Ark of the Testament, and behold the cherubim and the rest in their real nature."

And a very serious difficulty lies in the way of the popular assumption that the Vail of the Most Holy was rent in twain at the death of the Lord; for the Most Holy of the Temple, at the time of Christ, was divided from the Holy Place by two Vails, with a space of an ell or cubit between them.

The testimony of the *Mishna* is circumstantial and clear on this point. It says, that on the day of Atonement the High Priest "took the censer in his right hand, and a vial full of incense in his left. And he passed through the Temple till he came to the two Vails which separated the

Holy Place from the Most Holy, between which two Vails there was a space of an ell. . . . . The outer of these vails was raised at the south side, the inner 0n the north. He *stept in between them* . . . then turning to the left, passed along the inner Vail. . . . and setting down the censer . . . . poured the incense upon it, and waited till the whole Temple was filled with the smoke of the incense." (*Iom.* v. sec. 1.)

Note H

But if two Veils concealed the Most Holy from the Holy Place, the rending of one vail opened not the inner sanctuary either for the ingress or the gaze of priest or people. Yet this opening of the Most Holy is the very object for which the false assertion is made. Lightfoot felt this difficulty, and assumed that both the Vails concealing the Most Holy were rent at the crucifixion; but this is most unwarrantable, for the Synoptics speak expressly of one Vail only, when telling us "that the Vail of the Temple was rent in twain." (Matthew 27:51; Mark 15:38; Luke 23:45)

The Syriac Gospels are even more explicit:

"The front of the door of the Temple was rent from the midst of it."
Cureton's Remains (Luke 23:4-5)

At the entrance from the Court into the Holy Place there hung but one Vail; and as the golden doors before it were always open in the day time, the rending of that Vail would indeed unbare the Holy Place before the countless multitudes who on that evening thronged the Court for the offering of festive sacrifices. And a frank and unbiassed consideration of Matthew 27:50-54 and Luke 23:44-48 all but forces on one's mind the conviction that among the fearful prodigies which are related there as having been seen "by the people that came together to that sight, beholding the things that were done," was also the sudden tearing asunder of the Vail, which could only have been the case on Origen's view—viz., that the Vail of the Holy Place was then rent in twain.

Note I

"Do not ye after their works:
For they say and do not.
They .... enlarge the border of their garments."
(Matthew 23:3-5)

Note J

The symbolical meaning of these colors of the Vail was acknowledged in antiquity. Thus Josephus:

> "Nor was this mixture of colors without its mystical interpretation."

That he should have been ignorant of the true import of these colors is not wonderful, for he was ignorant of Christ, the Master-Key to these mysteries. Hence, he continues:

> "The colors were a kind of image of the universe; for by the scarlet there seemed to be enigmatically signified fire, by the fine flax the earth, by the blue the air, and by the purple the sea." Wars, v. 5.

Note K

The Jews invoke the dead, and plead their merits with God. The earliest allusion to this practice occurs in the Chaldee Paraphrase of Jonathan (Leviticus 9:2-3), said to have been written shortly before our era.

7

Jerusalem the Golden Foreshadowed by the Holy of Holies

The Tabernacle as a Type of the House of God in the Sense both of a Community and as Local Habitation

We have seen before that the Most Holy of the Tabernacle consisted of a cube, and was therefore marked by its very dimensions as a place of cosmical perfection.

And this circumstance was probably enhanced by the fact that it was a cube of ten cubits—and ten being regarded, as was said before, as the fully developed or perfected four—it would thus appear as the emphatic symbol of created order and beauty.

And the Heavenly Jerusalem also is described as bearing this cosmical symbol, for St. John says:

> "And the city lieth *four-square*,
> And the length is as large as the breadth:
> And he measured the city with the reed,
> Twelve thousand fur-longs.

The length and the breath, and the height of it.
Are equal." (Revelation 21:16)

The Most Holy Place in Solomon's Temple

On the subject of this holy city, Bengel, the author of the Gnomon, says "Let us not take its description in too material a sense, as though it were all literal, neither let us suppose it to be altogether figurative."

The existence of the city itself is matter of fact. This fact forms the substratum of those magnificent visions in the closing chapters of the Apocalypse, exactly in the same manner as the Being of Christ forms the substratum of the visions of the Lamb that had seven horns and seven eyes, or of the warrior with drawn sword riding forth to battle at the head of his spirit-hosts. The form of the Lamb, the seven horns and eyes, are emblems of character and attributes, and are obviously figurative; but underlying these emblems is the real Christ, possessed of the character and attributes which those serve to indicate.

Precisely as those emblems imply the real Christ, so do—the various features of the holy city imply the existence of a corresponding reality. Its walls and gates of pearl, its foundations of precious jewels, its streets of gold, are figurative; not so the underlying fact of its existence. And if the fact that the word "city" means in this instance a local sphere, may not be argued satisfactorily from the Apocalypse, there are other unfigurative passages of Holy Scripture in which the existence of such a local habitation is very plainly stated. The apostle Paul says, in reference to the patriarch Abraham,

> "By faith he sojourned in the land of promise,
> As in a strange country;
> Dwelling in tabernacles
> With Isaac and Jacob,
> The heirs with him of the same promise,
> For he looked for a city
> Which hath foundations,
> Whose builder and maker is God." (Hebrews 11:9-10)

To the saints of the New Testament, he says:

> "Ye are come
> Unto the City of the living God,
> The heavenly Jerusalem." (Hebrews 12:22)

And again: —

> "Here we have no continuing city,
> But we seek one to come." (Hebrews 13:14)

It is therefore both in keeping with the genius of the Apocalypse, and according to the analogy of other plain declarations in Holy Scripture, to conclude that St. John's descriptions of the Heavenly Jerusalem imply its real existence, while its details must be regarded as emblematical. Of the latter description is the cubical shape of the Holy City, denoting, as we have seen, the highest created beauty and order.

A City of Gold

Both in the Tabernacle and in Solomon's Temple, the Most Holy Place was overlaid with fine gold; and of the Heavenly Jerusalem it is said—

> "The city was pure gold, Like unto clear glass." (Revelation 21:18)

Gold, the Cabalists regarded as emblematical of the fire of the Divine essence; but who would venture to follow them in these trackless and tremendous speculations?

The Cherubim, which Moses and Solomon made of gold, Ezekiel sees in vision, as if made of fire. He says:

> "As for the likeness of the living creatures,
> Their appearance was like burning coals of fire;
> And the fire was bright,

And out of the fire went forth lightning;
And the living creatures
Ran and returned
As the appearance of a flash of lightning." (Ezekiel 1:13-14)

Whether the Cherubim which appeared to Moses in the Mount were in like manner of fire cannot be affirmed or denied.

But God's throne also, which in the Tabernacle was represented of fine gold was seen in vision,

"Like the fiery flame,
And his wheels as burning fire." (Daniel 7:9)

If then what is represented in divine art of gold, appears in vision as of fire, the Cabalists may be right in saying that there is some mystic resemblance between fire and gold.

And the red, transparent gold of the heavenly city may possibly combine the brilliancy and splendor of both, and as its cubical shape foreshadowed the exceeding beauty which is to distinguish it, *so the pure gold, like unto clear glass*, may denote the imperishable and glorified substance of which it is constructed. (*See Note A*)

The Tree of Life in the City

On the beautiful curtain that hung over the Tabernacle, foliage and cherubim were represented. In Solomon's Temple a development, as has been said before, of the Tabernacle, the king was commanded to sculpture on the interior cedar walls, and to overlay with fine gold lilies and palm-trees. The palm-tree is probably the symbol of the tree of life, and is called by this name in some tropical countries where its importance is best known. (*See Humboldt's Travels, p. 112*)

In a soil where nothing else can thrive, and under a scorching sun which burns up all other herbage, it rises, as if in triumphant defiance of some malignant opposition, to a marvelous height, and stretches out its evergreen luxuriant foliage for shade and shelter.

Some of its species afford "victum et amictum"—food and clothing—producing fruit, flour, wine, and thread to weave nets and garments, and from its stem a delicious and refreshing wine is drawn.

Its great beauty and manifold comforts have rendered its name a fond female appellation in the East: the life of whole tribes depends on this glorious tree, and probably because it is also known to resist unharmed the most terrible storms, it is a well-known Scriptural as well as ancient Pagan symbol of victory. It cannot be the tree of life, but it certainly is no unmeaning earthly symbol of it, and as the Most Holy of the Temple was filled with palm trees, so it is said of the Heavenly Jerusalem:

> "In the midst of the street of it,
> And on either side of the river,
> Was the tree of life,
> Which bare twelve manner of fruits,
> And yielded her fruit every month:
> And the leaves of the tree
> Were for the healing of the nations." (Revelation 22:2)

The Throne of God in the City

In the Most Holy Place of the Tabernacle rested the Ark of the Covenant—the symbolic Throne of God. It was called the Ark of His Covenant, evidently because He had solemnly covenanted, as the consummation of His love to Israel and Judah, to make His eternal Throne on Mount Zion.

Hence Jeremiah:

> "Hast thou utterly rejected Judah?
> Hath Thy soul loathed Zion?
> Do not abhor,
> For Thy name's sake!
> Do not disgrace the throne of My Glory,
> Remember,
> Break not Thy Covenant with us." (Jeremiah 14:19, 21)

Of that crowning act of His love, His presence on the Ark was pledge and partial fulfilment—partial, because this presence was concealed from the nation, and unapproachable to them: whereas His final session on Mount Zion should be in their very midst, and visible to all, as it is written:

> "Then
> The moon shall be confounded,
> And the sun ashamed,
> When the Lord shall reign
> In Mount Zion,
> And in the sight of His ancients gloriously." (Isaiah 24:23)

When the deepening sinfulness of the nominal Church seemed to obscure this high promise, the Prophet cries in sorrow,

> "Hath Thy soul loathed Zion?
> Do not disgrace the Throne of Thy Glory!" (Jeremiah 13:19-21)

But even at a period of still deeper sin, the Merciful, pointing to Jerusalem, repeats His ancient promise:

> "Son of Man,
> The place of My Throne,

And the place of the soles of My feet!
Where I will dwell
In the midst of the children of Israel forever!" (Ezekiel 43:7)

Of this final act of mercy the Ark appears to have been the sign and pledge.

It is not strange, therefore, that it should have been precious to the people, nor even that they should have taken it with them to battle, not as an idol-charm, as their enemies may have supposed, but as God's and their hosts' remembrancer.

Its presence appealed to Heaven for the protection of the holy city, and nerved the Jewish warrior as a pledge of victory.

But the loss of the Ark was, as it were, the loss of their highest national promise. Hence the marked consternation of Eli when he heard of its capture, which must have seemed to him the transfer of Israel's glory to the uncircumcised. Not the terrible tidings of the death of his two only sons, nor of the discomfiture of the Hebrew host, but the news of the capture of the Ark broke his heart.

> "It came to pass
> When the messenger made mention of the Ark of God,
> That he fell from off his seat backward . . .
> And his neck brake,
> And he died." (1 Samuel 4:18)

His daughter-in-law shared his patriotic grief and his tragic end.

"Ichabod!" she cried, as her soul went out of her,

"Ichabod! the glory is departed from Israel,
For the Ark of God is taken." (1 Samuel 4:18, 22)

But, true to the perversity of human nature, the merely nominal subjects of the ancient economy soon heeded the sign to the neglect and forgetfulness of the higher reality.

This great evil, in regard to the Ark, seems to have culminated in Jeremiah's time, who is said to have hid the Ark without telling where; and he almost pours contempt upon it, as a sign utterly abused, as Isaiah had poured contempt on festivals and sacrifices, and Hezekiah on the brazen serpent.

At the same time he bids the people to look forward to the promised period when in their holy city there should be seen the reality and fulfilment of what the Ark had symbolized.

He says—

"In those days, saith the Lord,
They shall say no more,
The Ark of the Covenant of the Lord:
Neither shall it come to mind:
Neither shall they remember it;
Neither shall they visit it;
Neither shall that be done any more;
At that time,
They shall call Jerusalem the Throne of the Lord,
And all the nations
Shall be gathered into it." (Jeremiah 3:16-17)

And as in the Most Holy Place rested the sign and pledge of God's Throne, so in the Heavenly Jerusalem, probably on the very site of the earthly to mark the literal fulfilment of the symbolical prophecy, God's glorious throne shall stand for ever.

> "There shall be no more curse;
> But the throne of God . . .
> Shall be in it." (Revelation 22:3, 5)

A Symbol of Christ

On the symbolical throne, the ark, lay the Mercy Seat, which the apostle Paul declares to be a symbol of Christ when he says:

> "All have sinned,
> And come short of the Glory of God;
> Being justified freely by His Grace
> Through the redemption that is in Christ Jesus
> Whom God has manifested as the Mercy Seat."

Theodoret says: "The Lord Jesus Christ is the true Mercy Seat;" and Olshausen: "As the Mercy Seat of the Tabernacle presented itself to the spirits of the people as the place from which forgiveness of their sins proceeded; so also is the Redeemer solemnly presented in the Holy of Holies of the universe to the believing gaze of that spiritual Israel which is gathered out of all nations, in order that they may receive forgiveness of their sins through His blood." (*So, Theodoret, Theophyl., Grotius, Olshausen.*)

And as the symbol of Christ rested on the ark—the type of Zion—so in that Golden City the Savior is enthroned:

> "And there shall be no more curse;
> But the throne of . . . the Lamb shall be in it." (Revelation 22:3)

Cherubim of Glory

At the two extremities of the Mercy Seat Moses placed the two Cherubim of glory: they were wrought out of the matter of the Mercy Seat, and were thus inseparably united with it. The gold of the Mercy Seat and of the Cherubim had lain together and been melted and fused together in the refiner's fiery crucible, and the Scriptures take pains to inform us that they were made of *beaten work*.

"Many a blow and biting sculpture" from the ponderous hammer in the artificer's anxious, but skillful hand, and countless lighter strokes—each blow, each lighter stroke reverberating tremulously, but inevitably and faithfully through the Mercy Seat itself—were needed, yes, imperatively needed, to produce these high ideal forms, to perfect the Divine beauty of their countenances, their polished limbs and airy plumage; to fix them face to face, and to give them their inclination, full of joy and wonder, towards the Mercy Seat from which they had risen. Suffering, fiery, sharp, and long, but effective victorious suffering, according to a Divine plan, and shared by the living Savior, was thus indicated, and when Solomon added two other Cherubim to complete the mystic four, he made them of olive wood—bitter, but oil or light-penetrated wood—to claim their kinship with the others made of beaten work.

But who are these Cherubim that are partakers of the Divine nature (2 Peter 1:4) that are united to Christ in inseparable union, and with Him are seated on that throne of eternal and universal rule? Can there be more than one answer? (*See Note B*)

The Savior Himself replies:

> "To him that overcometh
> Will I grant to sit with Me
> In my throne,
> Even as I also overcame

> And am set down with my Father
> In His throne." (Revelation 3:21)

No other created being shares that throne with Christ—none save His redeemed saints, and this fact so clearly and expressly stated, might, if it were necessary, bear the whole stress of the inquiry on this subject—these, and only these, the Cherubim were intended to foreshadow.

But the path to the throne lies through the Court and the Holy Place, and because flesh and blood finds that path often so hard and thorny, and would fain linger or even turn back again, He sends many bitter trials—sickness, disappointments, bereavements, orphanage, and widowhood—to urge us pilgrims on to the heavenly, golden termination.

Yet suffers He with His suffering children, for it is written:

> "In all their affliction
> He was afflicted." (Isaiah 63:9)

And

> "He that touched you,
> Touched the apple of His eye." (Zechariah 2:8)

But it may be asked:

What mean then the Cherubim which crowded the Most Holy Place, as they appeared on the curtain that formed its ceiling, and covered its northern and southern walls, and on the beautiful Vail which separated it from the Holy Place? And not the Most Holy only, but also the roof of the Holy Place, its western end and its two sides?

And in Solomon's Temple, confessedly but the development of the Tabernacle, they appeared moreover on the golden doors of the Holy Place, and on the Lavers in the Court. I reply:

As on the Mercy Seat, so everywhere else where the Cherubim are represented in the Tabernacle or the Temple, they are seen in union with the symbol of Christ—thus on the Vail of the Most Holy, the lowermost of the four curtains, and the Laver.

(1.)

It has been stated before, that the Vail of the Most Holy was in mystic dimensions, material, and the colors of its embroidery, identical with the Vail of the Holy Place; and since the latter has been shown to be the Shadow of Christ, it may be very fairly assumed that the former also, so essentially like it, foreshadowed Him.

In two points the Vails differed, viz.: the Vail of the Most Holy was of costlier workmanship than the other; and it also had the Cherubim, which the other lacked.

But the richer embroidery of the Vail of the Most Holy, if the type of Christ, would simply denote that He had now risen to a higher state of glory than that which He possessed, or chose to possess, when His holy flesh was rent upon the Cross.

With this conclusion the facts of the case entirely agree; and were foreshadowed, as has been seen, by the golden and crowned altar of incense as contrasted with the uncrowned brazen altar of sacrifice.

And the circumstance that the Cherubim appear on the Vail of the Most Holy, but not on the Vail which was torn, shows only the wonderful precision of these types: for although the members of Christ, if I may venture the expression, participated legally or judicially in His death, and were in Him when He accomplished it; yet were they not actually slain with Him, which would have been foreshadowed if the Vail that was rent had borne Cherubim upon it.

And the fact that the Cherubim are organically one with the Vail, is only another form exhibiting the great reality of their mystic union with it, set forth in many other ways, and especially on the Mercy Seat over the Ark.

(2.)

But if it be said that the Cherubim, being embroidered, as they were, in the same mystic colors which have been interpreted as emblems of the Savior's divine and human natures, would thus be shown to be partakers of both, I reply again:

Christ's living members are partakers of the whole Christ—a great and solemn fact in redemption this, which was not merely shown forth by the Shewbread on the Golden Table, and the Cherubim on the Mercy Seat, but is dogmatically stated by the Apostles, who declare that Christ's true members are not only members of His flesh (Ephesiahs 5:30), but are renewed in the image of *Him that created* them (Colossians 3:10); are changed into His image from glory to glory (2 Corinthians 3:8); shall be like Him (1 John 3:2); and still more explicitly, are called "to be partakers of the Divine nature" (2 Peter 1:4).

In this manner the Vail of the Most Holy uttered its profound symbolical lessons only in accordance with the other types of the Tabernacle, and the rest of Scripture, in exhibiting the Cherubim in union with the Lord.

(3.)

The lowermost of the four curtains was of the same texture, colors, costly embroidery, and design, as the Vail of the Most Holy, and must therefore have been meant to convey the same great lessons.

Of the same import also was the fact that the Cherubim were represented on the Lavers in Solomon's Temple. As time went on, the truths of Redemption stood out with increasing clearness, and it became known that at the very commencement of the Divine life, the possessor of that life was in union with his Lord—the Laver being, as has been said, an early shadow of Christ—and was possessed in God's eye of the characteristics which the Cherubim were meant to convey.

Into these characteristics I cannot enter now, as a separate book would be required to state them with clearness and precision. But thus, much must be said, that as the glory of Christ was revealed with increasing fulness as the dispensations advanced towards the consummation, that of the Cherubim kept pace with it.

Hence in the Court of the Temple they were, like Him, represented in brass; in the Holy Place, in fine linen and embroidery; and in the Most Holy, again like Him, in massive gold.

I have said before, but it is a matter of feeling—the feeling of concinnity (harmonious arrangment) and congruity rather than a thought that can be logically stated—that the Cherubim on the Vail and Curtain, and those on the bas-reliefs in the Temple which took the place of the Curtain, exhibited a less advanced state than the Cherubim of massive gold, and standing forth in perfect forms on the Mercy Seat; but such is my impression: and it appears to be confirmed by the fact, that only those Cherubim on the Mercy Seat are called the Cherubim of the Glory.

(4.)

But it may still be objected, that the Cherubim on the Vail appear also in the Most Holy, which foreshadowed the Heavenly Jerusalem. Is it, then, to be expected that a mingling of the less and the most perfect of Christ's members is to take place in the golden city? Yes, certainly.

The Most Holy of the Tabernacle is the type of the heavenly Jerusalem; the glorious city of the blest come down from heaven to earth. But at the period of its descent the whole earth will not yet be changed into its likeness; that will come to pass at the end of a given period—the period described under the probably symbolical number of a thousand years.

In the meantime the surrounding world is not yet glorified, nor its inhabitants, who will then resemble the true Christian of the present dispensation in all essential characteristics.

But the inhabitants of the earth shall walk in the light of the Heavenly Jerusalem, shall eat the leaves of the tree of life, and bring their honor and glory into the golden city.

Hence there must be Cherubim represented there, besides the perfect ones on the throne—Cherubim of a less glorious degree, crowding and filling it. (*"The gates of it shall not be shut at all by day, For there shall be no night there. And they shall bring the glory and honor of the nations into it." Revelation 21:25*)

But, as in the Mosaic Most Holy Place the Cherubim, the symbols of God's saints, are seen in union with the Mercy Seat, so in the Golden City the saints themselves are enthroned with Christ, and abide with Him on that throne forever.

The Shekinah Glory

On the Ark, over the Mercy Seat, and between the Cherubim, rested the Shekina, or the Cloud of the Glory of God. (Leviticus 16:12-13)

But on the throne in the Heavenly Jerusalem, the Father also will appear in majesty in the midst of the glorified Church.

> "He showed me a pure river of water of life,
> And there shall in no wise enter into it
> Anything that defiled,
> Neither whatsoever worketh abomination,
> Or market a lie:
> But they which are written in the Lamb's Book of Life." (Revelation 21:27)

And . . . . .

> "In the midst of the street of it,
> And on either side of the river,
> Was the tree of life,
> Which bare twelve manner of fruits,
> And yielded her fruit every month,
> And the leaves of the tree were for the healing of the nations. . .
> Blessed are they that do His commandments,
> That they may have right to the tree of life,
> And may enter in through the gates into the city."
> (Revelation 22:2, 14)
> "Clear as crystal,
> Proceeding out of the flame of God and of the Lamb."
> (Revelation 22:1)
> "Behold, the Tabernacle of God is with men,
> And He will dwell with them,

And they shall be His people,
And God Himself shall be with them."
(Revelation 21:3)

And as the Presence of God in symbol was the only source of light in the Most Holy, so His Real Presence is the light of the heavenly city, as it is said:

"There shall be no night there;
And they need no candle,
Neither light of the sun,
For the Lord God giveth them light;
And they shall reign for ever and ever."
(Revelation 22:5)

And again:

"And the city had no need of the sun,
Neither of the moon, to shine in it:
For the glory of God did lighten it,
And the Lamb is the light thereof.
And the nations of them that are saved
Shall walk in the light of it."
(Revelation 21:23-24)

These points of analogy, which it would be easy to multiply, between the Most Holy of the Tabernacle and the Heavenly Jerusalem, are too accurate and striking to be merely accidental; and the resemblance between an almost neglected type of the Old Testament, and those grandest visions of the New, admits but of one sensible explanation as to its origin, and that is,—*design*.

God *designed* that the Most Holy should be a symbol, or standing visible prophecy, of the Church's exalted consummation.

Note A

The imperishable wood which Moses placed between the inner and outer plates of gold, in the walls of the Holy and Most Holy, may have foreshadowed the same elements "that cannot be moved or destroyed" (Hebrews 12:26-26); and the fact that the golden plates and wood were used for the Holy Place as well as the Most Holy, is deeply significant, for the elements of the future glorious world probably form even now the basis of our earth.

Note B

The Scriptural proof that the cherubim represent the saints is extremely simple.

The first step in the argument is to show that cherubim and living creatures are identical beings.

This proof is supplied by Ezekiel. After describing the living creatures and mystic wheels which he had seen in holy vision by the river Chebar, the Prophet says:

> "This is the living creature
> That I saw under the God of Israel
> By the river Chebar;
> And I knew that they were the cherubim." (Ezekiel 10:20)

Indeed, throughout the tenth chapter he speaks of the same beings as cherubim, which in the first he had called living creatures.

The second step is to show that the living creatures of Ezekiel, and the apostle John's four beasts, also are identical beings.

This is done not only by comparing their general likeness—the four faces of lion, bull, man, and eagle—their wings, and especially their position in the immediate presence of God and his Throne; but by establishing the fact that their names are strictly identical. The Greeks call them both Zoa, which merely by an oversight King James's translators could have rendered "living creatures" in Ezekiel, and "beasts" in the book of John.

But if living creatures are cherubim, and John's four beasts are living creatures, it follows they also are cherubim.

The next step is to inquire into their meaning. This we gather from their own lips:

> "And when he had taken the book, the four cherubim
> And four-and-twenty elders fell down before the Lamb,
> Having every one of them harps, and golden vials full of odours,
> Which are the prayers of the saints.
> And they sung a new song, saying,
> Thou art worthy to take the book,
> And to open the seals thereof;
> For thou wast slain
> And hast redeemed us to God by Thy blood,
> Out of every kindred, and tongue, and people, and nation,
> And hast made us unto our God kings and priests,
> And 'we shall reign on the earth." (Revelation 5:8-10)

It is evident, therefore, from their own confession, in which no angel joins—and very different is the hymn of the angelic host, as recorded in the same chapter, for they make no allusion to their redemption through blood—that they, the cherubim, as well as the elders, are redeemed men.

Beautifully says Hildebert of Le Mans, in confirmation of this view:

> "Each righteous man contains these symbols four.
> For *human* sense he claims the human face;
> The ox in self-denial finds a place;
> *Lion* is he as conqueror in hard straits;
> *Eagle*, for oft he seeks the heavenly gates."

Gregory the Great also says:

> "Each good man has within him that which is signified by the four living creatures, inasmuch as all goodness in God's saints consists in their resemblance to the Son of God."